Praise for

Scattered Minds

"Well organized and comprehensive, this is sure to become a valuable resource."

—*Library Journal*

"Balanced and highly informative, grounded in science, yet conveyed with his extraordinary bedside manner and sensitivity to the clinical needs of these adults. Well done, Dr. Adler."

—Russell A. Barkley, Ph.D., Research Professor of Psychiatry, SUNY Upstate Medical University

"A welcome addition to the literture about adult attention deficit hyperactivity disorder (ADHD) . . . Len Adler is well-known as both a clinical expert in ADHD and a regular contributor to the research literature on the topic. It thus comes as no surprise that the book combines clinical wisdom with empirical data in a manner that will be interesting, useful, and accessible for clinicians who treat ADHD and for patients seeking accurate and up-to-date information about the disorder."

—Steven V. Faraone, Ph.D., Director, Medical Genetics Research; Professor of Psychiatry and of Neuroscience and Physiology; Director, Child and Adolescent Psychiatry Research, SUNY Upstate Medical University

"*Scattered Minds* is both accessible and readable. Whether you use it as a reference or read it cover to cover, it will enhance your bookshelf as you collect resources about ADHD."

—Alan R. Graham, Ph.D., co-owner of ADDvisor

"After reading this book, people with symptoms of ADHD should find comfort knowing that there are ways to live a very normal and successful life with ADHD."

—Danielle Fisher, youngest American to climb Mt. Everest and youngest person (age 20) in the world to climb the seven summits

SCATTERED MINDS

Hope and Help for Adults with
Attention Deficit Hyperactivity Disorder

LENARD ADLER, M.D.
with Mari Florence

A PERIGEE BOOK

A PERIGEE BOOK
Published by the Penguin Group
Penguin Group (USA) Inc.
375 Hudson Street, New York, New York 10014, USA
Penguin Group (Canada), 90 Eglinton Avenue East, Suite 700, Toronto, Ontario M4P 2Y3,
Canada (a division of Pearson Penguin Canada Inc.)
Penguin Books Ltd., 80 Strand, London WC2R 0RL, England
Penguin Group Ireland, 25 St. Stephen's Green, Dublin 2, Ireland (a division of Penguin Books Ltd.)
Penguin Group (Australia), 250 Camberwell Road, Camberwell, Victoria 3124, Australia
(a division of Pearson Australia Group Pty. Ltd.)
Penguin Books India Pvt. Ltd., 11 Community Centre, Panchsheel Park, New Delhi—110 017, India
Penguin Group (NZ), 67 Apollo Drive, Mairangi Bay, Auckland 1311, New Zealand
(a division of Pearson New Zealand Ltd.)
Penguin Books (South Africa) (Pty.) Ltd., 24 Sturdee Avenue, Rosebank, Johannesburg 2196,
South Africa

Penguin Books Ltd., Registered Offices: 80 Strand, London WC2R 0RL, England

While the author has made every effort to provide accurate telephone numbers and Internet addresses
at the time of publication, neither the publisher nor the author assumes any responsibility for er-
rors, or for changes that occur after publication. Further, the publisher does not have any control
over and does not assume any responsibility for author or third-party websites or their content.

PRINTING HISTORY
G. P. Putnam's Sons hardcover edition / May 2006
Perigee trade paperback edition / May 2007

Perigee trade paperback ISBN: 978-0-399-53340-2

The Library of Congress has cataloged the Putnam hardcover edition as follows:

Adler, Lenard.
    Scattered minds: hope and help for adults with attention
    deficit hyperactivity disorder / Lenard Adler.
    p.   cm.
    Includes index.
    ISBN 0-399-15361-6
    1. Attention deficit disorder in adults.   2. Attention deficit hyperactivity disorder.
    I. Title.
RC394.A85A345   2006   2005056681

PRINTED IN THE UNITED STATES OF AMERICA
10 9 8 7 6 5 4 3 2 1

PUBLISHER'S NOTE: Neither the publisher nor the author is engaged in rendering professional
advice or services to the individual reader. The ideas, procedures, and suggestions contained in this
book are not intended as a substitute for consulting with your physician. All matters regarding your
health require medical supervision. Neither the author nor the publisher shall be liable or responsible for any loss or damage allegedly arising from any information or suggestion in this book.

Most Perigee Books are available at special quantity discounts for bulk purchases for sales promotions, premiums, fund-raising, or educational use. Special books, or book excerpts, can also be
created to fit specific needs. For details, write: Special Markets, Penguin Group (USA) Inc., 375
Hudson Street, New York, New York 10014.

Acknowledgments

A number of individuals over the years have been instrumental in my professional development and my understanding of adult attention deficit hyperactivity disorder (adult ADHD).

First and foremost, I would like to thank my patients. They have been gracious with their time and sharing their life stories with me. Their willingness to discuss their life experiences has been critical in furthering my understanding of adult ADHD. Their stories also form the backbone of this book.

My colleagues in the departments of psychiatry and neurology at the New York University School of Medicine, particularly Dr. John Rotrosen and the team at the Mental Health and Addictive Disorders Research Program, deserve special mention for their support over the last twenty-four years.

My cowriter, Mari Florence, has been instrumental in "finding the right words" and always making herself available to meet our deadlines. Her interns, Barbara Jarvik and Jennifer Chang, were quite helpful in conducting some of the background research.

A special note of thanks goes out to my editor, Marian Lizzi, and her team at Penguin. She provided the initial impetus for this endeavor and a steady hand throughout the writing. The final product that follows would not have been possible without her wisdom and counsel.

Last, I would like to acknowledge my parents, who provided ongoing support during my postgraduate education. My family, as always, has been incredibly understanding in lending their encouragement and in giving me the time needed to complete this endeavor.

To Rhonda

Contents

Foreword

I can't adequately describe what getting the diagnosis of attention deficit disorder (ADD) has done for me. To say that it has changed my life would be a gross understatement. Finding out about ADD and getting treatment for it have indeed given me a new life, even at my somewhat advanced age of fifty-nine. I just wish the average adult knew about this condition, and I wish the facts were more widely understood."

This comment, sent to me by a man in Michigan, resembles the literally tens of thousands of similar messages, letters, and e-mails I have received over the twenty-five years I have been treating attention deficit disorder. While the general public still widely thinks of ADD as a childhood condition, the greatest proportion of the grateful messages I receive come from adults.

These adults had been languishing prior to finding out about ADD. They had been living under the curse of what I call the "moral diagnosis." Terms like "bad," "lazy," or "incompetent" had plagued them for most of their lives, terms that served no constructive purpose but did do the dirty, socially sanctioned work of morally judging these individuals, thus deepening the feelings of ineptitude, hopelessness, and despair with which so many of them slogged on through life, bravely bearing disappointment after disappointment and fencing with frustration after frustration.

Some adults with undiagnosed ADD lose the battle, in drug overdose, in violent crime, in car accidents, in prison, in reckless and dangerous behavior. But most survive, only to struggle with ongoing frustration and underachievement year after year.

This does not have to be. The darkness of the world of the moral diagnosis can and now ought to give way to the light of the medical diagnosis. What a bright new day knowledge—supplanting judgment—can create.

Now, as we understand the mind in terms of biology rather than morality, in terms of science rather than voodoo, in terms of reason rather than superstition, the stigma and fear that used to surround mental and physical differences are—very gradually—dissipating. One good example is the diagnosis of attention deficit disorder.

The diagnosis of ADD in an adult is a particularly dramatic event because it can reverse decades of suffering, decades of underachievement, frustration, lost jobs, fractured relationships, low self-regard, and a host of other problems that proper diagnosis and treatment can address.

There are very few diagnoses in all of medicine that carry with them as much realistic hope for improvement as does the diagnosis of ADD in an adult. The major obstacle is that most people—including many doctors—do not know much about the condition, nor do they know how to diagnose it or treat it.

Enter this excellent book. Dr. Len Adler, researcher and clinician extraordinaire, has composed a superb introduction to ADD in adults that he has aptly titled *Scattered Minds*. But this book is anything but scattered. Whether you are a professional or a layperson, this book will give you all you need to know, laid out in clear and well-organized prose.

I believe that as you read this book, you will also gain hope and enthusiasm. A better life awaits millions of adults, and the first step is to read and understand the information you hold in your hands.

Edward M. Hallowell, M.D.,
coauthor of *Driven to Distraction,*
Delivered from Distraction,
and author of *CrazyBusy*

"Stop, Look, and Listen"

This book is the culmination of ten years of working with adults with ADHD and related disorders. As director of the Adult ADHD program at New York University, I have been involved in myriad studies relating to the disorder, and I played a role in creating screening and diagnostic tools that help identify the condition with accuracy. Along with my colleagues and many inspiring patients, I have worked to find new ways to manage the condition, which you will read about in this book.

I do not have ADHD myself, and I did not grow up with and go to medical school with a driving desire to study this disorder. However, very early on in my professional career, I saw how adults with ADHD were suffering and weren't getting an accurate diagnosis or proper treatment because this condition was considered solely a childhood illness. I saw that these adults struggled at work, at home, and in their social interactions with others. Some described symptoms of inattention—they were easily distracted and had trouble paying attention and staying organized—while others had trouble with the hyperactivity and impulsivity that sometimes mark the condition (they were often restless, fidgety, unable to slow down, and would speak or act without thinking things through).

While the roots of ADHD are in childhood, the problems of these adults made it very clear that this neuropsychiatric disorder often continues into adulthood—in fact, two out of three children with ADHD go on to become adults with the disorder. These adults also made it clear that they wanted and needed help.

I have always felt that as a physician, I learn best when I listen to my patients, hear their stories, and let their words lead the way. Establishing symptoms and taking a history over the course of an individual's life is the cornerstone of clinical medicine, and it is often easy for physicians to forget this in their busy modern work schedules. It is easy to rely on laboratory or imaging tests (such as blood work or MRI scans) to help make the diagnosis for many illnesses. Unfortunately, for ADHD, the diagnostic blood work and imaging tests remain research tools. The only way to get a diagnosis is to sit down with your physician and talk about your life story—your symptoms and how they have affected your life. A patient of mine put it quite succinctly: "Stop, look, listen, and note your inattentive symptoms."

The best way to talk about the journey from pre-diagnosis to successful management is by sharing these stories. My patients have graciously allowed me to describe their experiences. I have changed their names, but the stories show how far they've come. Perhaps you will see yourself in some of these anecdotes.

Tim's story is a moving one—and highlights several important facts:

- ADHD is often overlooked in individuals who are successful in certain realms of their professional life.
- It is never too late to get diagnosed and treated—ADHD affects individuals throughout the life span.
- Effective treatment involves a partnership between patient and physician, not only in establishing the diagnosis, but also in selecting treatment and monitoring the response to medication.
- There are treatments available that can lead to meaningful changes; the first step is to obtain a diagnosis.
- Medications are the first-line treatment for ADHD, but they provide only the tools for you to make changes in your life. They can improve your symptoms—including difficulty paying attention, easy distraction, and drifting off in conversations and trouble remembering what has been said or read. Therapy and coaching offer additional help. We'll discuss the road to getting better later in the book.

Tim's Story

Tim is a sixty-three-year-old real estate entrepeneur who came to my office for an evaluation of a lifelong history of trouble completing things in a timely fashion and difficulty listening to others. He was referred by his fifteen-year-old son's pediatrician because, after participating in his son's evaluation for ADHD, he realized he had many of the same symptoms.

Tim was worried about whether his difficulty paying attention was due in part to hearing loss in one ear and he had first wanted to obtain an evaluation from an otolaryngologist (ENT physician) prior to seeing the ADHD specialist. However, he mixed up the physicians' names and specialties and came to my office to get a hearing evaluation.

Tim was surprised when I asked him to complete a survey of ADHD symptoms and then sit down and talk things over with me, without a hearing test. He was able to laugh at his mistake (as I discussed with him later, his confusing the physicians' names was a symptom of what had brought him to my office). His ability to use humor when dealing with his symptoms was a major asset that had served him well.

Tim's experience of being referred to me for an ADHD evaluation by his child's doctor is typical. Tim told me an interesting story of his current life situation. He described himself as a fairly successful real estate entrepreneur, but said he had great difficulty completing tasks in a timely fashion and that his difficulty planning had led to his missing out on several significant projects. Tim felt that he worked best for himself and that he would have difficulty working for others and following their instructions/timetables. He had no significant medical history except for the partial hearing loss, and had been in psychotherapy for several years for issues of trouble completing tasks and some marital discord. He had had one episode of depression several decades before, which subsided after about a month without treatment.

I'm including Tim's survey of ADHD symptoms, the Adult Self-Report Scale (ASRS) v1.1, as an example of what a symptom checklist looks like and what the eighteen symptoms of ADHD are. The ASRS v1.1 was established by a work group of experts on adult ADHD and is copyrighted by the World Health Organization (WHO). We'll take a closer look at this screening tool, which I was privileged to participate in developing, later in the book. For now, it's important to note that the first six items are the most predictive of ADHD.

Adult Self-Report Scale (ASRS v1.1) Symptom Checklist

Patient Name   **Today's Date**

Please answer the questions below, rating yourself on each of the criteria shown using the scale on the right side of the page. As you answer each question, place an X in the box that best describes how you have felt and conducted yourself over the past six months. Please give this completed checklist to your healthcare professional to discuss during today's appointment. Shaded areas indicate significant symptoms.

PART A

	NEVER	RARELY	SOMETIMES	OFTEN	VERY OFTEN
1. How often do you have trouble wrapping up the final details of a project, once the challenging parts have been done?	☐	☐	☒	☐	☐
2. How often do you have difficulty getting things in order when you have to do a task that requires organization?	☐	☐	☒	☐	☐
3. When you have a task that requires a lot of thought, how often do you avoid or delay getting started?	☐	☐	☐	☒	☐
4. How often do you have problems remembering appointments or obligations?	☐	☐	☐	☒	☐
5. How often do you fidget or squirm with your hands or feet when you have to sit down for a long time?	☐	☐	☒	☐	☐
6. How often do you feel overly active and compelled to do things, like you were driven by a motor?	☐	☐	☒	☐	☐

PART B

	NEVER	RARELY	SOMETIMES	OFTEN	VERY OFTEN
7. How often do you make careless mistakes when you have to work on a boring or difficult project?	☐	☐	☒	☐	☐

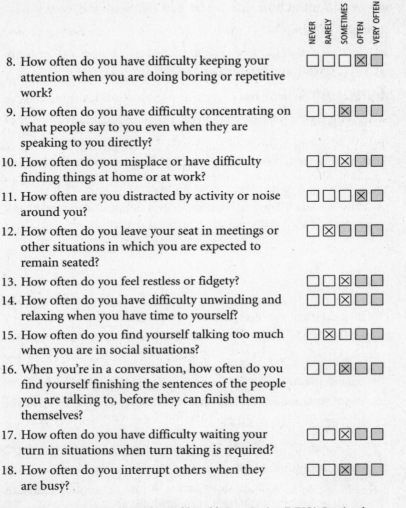

	NEVER	RARELY	SOMETIMES	OFTEN	VERY OFTEN
8. How often do you have difficulty keeping your attention when you are doing boring or repetitive work?	☐	☐	☐	☒	☐
9. How often do you have difficulty concentrating on what people say to you even when they are speaking to you directly?	☐	☐	☒	☐	☐
10. How often do you misplace or have difficulty finding things at home or at work?	☐	☐	☒	☐	☐
11. How often are you distracted by activity or noise around you?	☐	☐	☐	☒	☐
12. How often do you leave your seat in meetings or other situations in which you are expected to remain seated?	☐	☒	☐	☐	☐
13. How often do you feel restless or fidgety?	☐	☐	☒	☐	☐
14. How often do you have difficulty unwinding and relaxing when you have time to yourself?	☐	☐	☒	☐	☐
15. How often do you find yourself talking too much when you are in social situations?	☐	☒	☐	☐	☐
16. When you're in a conversation, how often do you find yourself finishing the sentences of the people you are talking to, before they can finish them themselves?	☐	☐	☒	☐	☐
17. How often do you have difficulty waiting your turn in situations when turn taking is required?	☐	☐	☒	☐	☐
18. How often do you interrupt others when they are busy?	☐	☐	☒	☐	☐

As you can see from Tim's ASRS Symptom Checklist, he showed significant symptoms of ADHD, inattention, and a few of the hyperactive-impulsive symptoms. You'll learn in the following chapters that ADHD symptoms can be divided into inattentive (items 1–4 and 7–11 on the checklist) and hyperactive-impulsive (items 5–6 and 12–18). A person can have inattentive and/or hyperactive-impulsive symptoms, with most having some of both; clearly you can have significant symptoms in only one subset, as is the case for Tim, who has seven out of nine significant inattentive symptoms. For a positive diagnosis, a person must have six out of nine of the symptoms significantly, in one or both categories.

Let's look at the symptoms that Tim described. These include difficulty finishing things, trouble organizing, procrastination, forgetfulness, trouble paying attention when doing something boring or repetitive, trouble concentrating when others are speaking, and being easily distracted.

Not only did Tim have the above symptoms of inattentive ADHD, but the symptoms were causing him difficulty at work and at home. He reported that his wife was becoming increasingly frustrated with his inability to complete tasks around the house and described him as "spacey." These issues were the driving force behind their previous visits to couples' therapy. At work, he felt he was inefficient and not performing at the level he was capable of. His difficulty planning—in spite of a daily planner—led him to take longer to finish projects than it should. His difficulty remembering what he had read also hampered his productivity.

Tim said that as a child, he had had similar problems with procrastination, planning, and remembering what others had said or what he had read. He felt that these symptoms had significantly affected his life and dated back to the first grade. The only other significant mental health issue was a brief episode of depression, but there were no signs of a mood disorder currently.

I told Tim that I felt he had ADHD, and we discussed treatment options, including medication. After a week to think things over, he agreed to start a trial of the non-stimulant atomoxetine (Strattera). Strattera was initiated and after slowly increasing the dosage over six weeks, he was stabilized at 35 mg in the morning and 25 mg in the evening. He has described a significant improvement in his ability to complete and stay on tasks, which is noticeable in his increased efficiency at work and at home.

Tim's improved attention span has been noticed by both his wife and his colleagues. He used a tennis analogy to describe how he is now able to plan better: Previously he could see a ball that was hit to him bounce, but would not be able to follow it until it hit his racquet. Now, he "can see the ball not only after it bounces but right into the racquet. . . . [The benefit is] that if you see the ball approach your racquet, you can make a last-second adjustment."

Tim feels that the pace of his thinking (what he calls "mind speed") has increased and that he is now much more aware of his symptoms and how to cope with them. He is trying to "stop, look, and listen" whenever he nears completion of a task or listens to others. This helps him to stay focused in conversations and to complete the detailed aspects of tasks.

Tim also recently went back to his therapist for a follow-up visit. He told me that his therapist also noticed a significant change in him. Where previously he had been resistant to suggestions, now he is more able to look at his actions and think about how he might change. Tim has been working hard at translating the improvement in his symptoms into meaningful changes in his home and work life and has been making significant progress in a relatively short period of time.

I'd like to share with you some passages from a note Tim recently sent me, describing his thoughts about being treated for ADHD. He entitled it "The Gift."

> When I last saw Dr. Adler, he assured me that there was more to come beyond mind speed. I could not imagine what that could be, and a few days later I realized it was a sense of well-being in the knowledge that mind speed was not something I would watch only from afar but could also experience myself.
>
> My thinking has now evolved to realize that I have been given a significant gift. It requires management and is not a reward in itself. It is just a tool. However, if I can seize this opportunity how to manage it . . . it may pay great dividends. If I am to take advantage of this gift, it must benefit not only me but others, starting with my wife.

I encourage you to read this book with Tim's success, and your own, in mind. Like him, you too are a uniquely gifted individual, and with proper care and symptom management, you too will be free to seek out and more fully enjoy the rewards your life has to offer.

CHAPTER ONE

What Is Adult ADHD?

You know something is wrong with your life, but how do you figure out what it is and what to do about it? Maybe a few things here and there keep going wrong and you're starting to wonder if it's just bad luck, these things happen to everyone, or perhaps time just seems to be rushing by faster than ever. Or, more likely, you've been struggling for some time now and, despite your best efforts, you can't manage your life with the ease that your friends and colleagues seem to. You feel fairly certain something isn't right.

You may have been directed to this book by a caring family member or a friend, or perhaps by your own inquisitiveness. You've tried to focus and probably feel that if you could just knuckle down, then you could keep up with your life—but you can't seem to get it together. Or maybe your child has just been diagnosed with ADHD and the pediatrician or child psychiatrist gently pointed out that it's often an inherited disorder. Perhaps after a series of workplace mishaps, someone unkindly suggested that you "deal with your ADD problem." No matter what direction you're coming from, considering ADHD as your reality is emotionally disturbing, and I empathize with you.

I've spent a great deal of my professional life studying ADHD and its treatments, and I can definitively tell you that it's a verifiable illness with a host of unpleasant and life-altering symptoms. In the following chapters I explain what happens when this imbalance occurs, how it affects your body and mind, and what you can do to feel better. The good news is that with a professional diagnosis and proper treatment, it can be managed effectively and your life can improve.

Throughout this book, I describe what adult attention deficit disorder (ADD), as well as attention deficit hyperactivity disorder (ADHD), is, and how it is successfully treated. (For the purposes of this book I use the term ADHD to refer to all attention deficit disorders.) This information is based on solid scientific study and my clinical practice over more than two decades. I share the true stories of some of my patients and other individuals who have been successfully treated for ADHD. Help is out there, and if you choose to accept it, you can get better.

Some of you won't need to read these early chapters to determine if you have ADHD. You've already made your own diagnosis and it's probably correct, although you'll need confirmation from your doctor. After everything is said and done, only you can decide if you need treatment, but after reading this you will know a lot more about your condition and how it affects you and those around you.

I devote pages in this book to describing the medications available, their benefits and side effects, and what you need to know before beginning treatment. Some adults who have ADHD-like symptoms don't have the condition, so I discuss other health conditions and syndromes that manifest similar symptoms and conditions that are often present alongside ADHD. There are also quite a few symptoms that aren't widely discussed outside the medical community, and I identify them and how they factor into your condition. In addition to the medications that are available, there are also many non-medical treatments that can be used in conjunction with medication, and some have such positive results that they are part of an overall strategy. I outline these and how they work as part of the complete plan. I also discuss alternative treatments that are often used, and while there is not much solid proof of their efficacy, you should know about them.

Lastly, the adult with ADHD has often burned many bridges and stumbled over many personal and professional obstacles over the years. I provide steps to rebuild relationships, address career mishaps, and improve the overall health of your life.

The treatment plan I outline is not complicated, but it can nonetheless present a challenge for the ADHD patient. I clearly understand that many of you have difficulty maintaining focus and remembering what you've just been told. I promise that I will make this book, and the explanations within, as clear and to-the-point as possible.

Where It Starts

Sue is a sixty-year-old former legal secretary who originally came to my office ten years ago because she suspected she had ADHD. She had read an article on ADHD and many of the symptoms struck a chord in her. Sue described a lifelong history of difficulty paying attention when reading and in conversation (which resulted in her not being able to remember parts of conversations and needing to reread passages to get the meaning of what she had just read), daydreaming, procrastinating, losing items, forgetfulness, trouble prioritizing and organizing tasks, and difficulty managing time such that she was almost always late for appointments. As a child she did not do well in elementary school, and throughout her academic endeavors teachers had often commented that she "was not trying" and performing to her potential. Sue felt that she underperformed on the job and that the issues of time management and forgetfulness were affecting her at home and socially. She had several close friends, but was somewhat socially isolated for reasons she could not fully explain.

Everybody has "one of those days" when things go wrong. You can't find your keys. You are looking for them and you start to think about where you might have left them, and then you are not paying attention when you are driving, and you have a minor fender bender in a parking lot. For adults with ADHD, every day is one of those days. Those individual stressors are much harder on a person with ADHD. The symptoms don't occur in a vacuum, but are context-based and will manifest when individuals are doing things that they don't like, don't want to do, or find challenging, such as completing a project under deadline or preparing for a test. While healthy people also sometimes struggle in these situations, stressful situations have much more of an impact on adults with ADHD.

For some individuals, ADHD impacts every part of their lives. Others are able to focus on tasks, but lose it on the minutiae of the day to day. To cap this all off, many are perceived as "scatterbrained" or "lazy" by family, peers, and employers. With or without a diagnosis, individuals with ADHD can be misperceived and thus negatively impacted by their condition.

At home, Sue's parents were often frustrated by her forgetfulness and her failure to complete tasks. She described a poignant instance from childhood where she was sent to her room to retrieve an item and remembered she had not brushed her teeth, so she went into the bathroom. She realized her hair needed brushing and then she could not remember why she had originally gone to the bathroom or to her room. This was a fairly typical incident from her childhood. Sue said she always thought something was wrong with her, but did not know what it was and chalked it up to being "stupid." As an adult, she was having increasing difficulty at work as she went from a situation in which she had a great deal of structure and autonomy in her work with her former employer, but her new boss ran the office on a tight schedule, which he imposed.

You may find that everyday stress exacerbates the situation. One day it gets to be too much, so you don't go to work. The next time you can't go in, you feel so guilty that you don't even call the office. Perhaps you drink a bit. You often feel confused, forgetful, and unable to concentrate, and you're always stressed and feel like you're at the end of your rope. You wake up tired every morning no matter how much sleep you've had the night before. By this time, nobody has to tell you that you haven't felt right in a long time.

You increasingly find yourself compensating for your shortcomings. Gradually and almost without realizing it, you stop making plans with your family and friends because they're always upset with you for being late or doing something wrong. Or perhaps people have stopped inviting you out. Sometimes you don't care, because you have no idea how you'll feel at the time anyway, but underneath, it hurts your feelings. Your life has fallen into an unpredictable, yet dull, routine, like a hamster in one of those giant Habitrail tunnels.

Your life has entered a vortex, a spiral that may include confusion, depression, and anxiety. For some, it may be a simple obstacle; for others it feels like rock bottom and you reproach yourself: It must all be due to your inadequacies or poor coping skills. You feel guilty for all the things you can't do and all the people you are letting down.

Relationships have suffered: Your family is less and less tolerant of your screwups. Your partner or significant other is easily frustrated with you. The realization that led you to this book is the fact that you've begun to worry about almost everything falling through the cracks. You want to be like everybody else. Perhaps you've contemplated just dropping out of society, or even suicide.

If you're lucky, someone has directed you toward ADHD, and in a compassionate way. If you're not, perhaps you had diagnostic tests that led nowhere and cost a great deal of money. Or your friends and relatives have suggested making lists and tapping into your self-discipline or perhaps taking nutritional supplements. They're well intentioned but, by now, we know that doesn't work.

Who Has Adult ADHD?

While you may have felt like an outcast for much of your life, or found yourself ostracized for your erratic behaviors, you're not alone. ADHD is a common and impairing disorder that often goes unrecognized and untreated because most individuals who have it don't know it, or if they know they don't seek treatment. While we're learning more and more about it every day, it is still grossly underdiagnosed and undertreated by patients and doctors alike.

While childhood ADHD is diagnosed at a ratio of about four boys to one girl, in adults it appears to affect men and women about two to one. As we age, hyperactivity becomes less of an issue and the cognitive challenges, such as forgetfulness and lack of concentration, emerge. Despite these changes, the condition tends not to mellow with age as two-thirds of children with ADHD go on to be adults with ADHD and experience constant and persistent obstacles.

ADHD is an equal-opportunity disorder, affecting all ethnic and socioeconomic groups. Untreated, the condition has serious consequences that affect all areas of your life. Two recent studies found that adults with ADHD are:

- 50 percent more likely to be currently unemployed;
- 75 percent more likely to change jobs;
- twice as likely to be arrested;
- twice as likely to be divorced;
- twice as likely to abuse alcohol and tobacco.[1, 2, 3]

Does this sound extreme? It is. One of the finer results of years of study and testing is that ADHD is finally being recognized for what it is: a hereditary and impairing neurological disorder. While my colleagues and I are determined to demystify this illness for the public and increase awareness of the efficacy of proper treatment, there are still many doctors and pediatricians out there who treat

ADHD as a "nuisance": a bit of hyperactivity combined with poor impulse control. But I assure you that it's anything but that.

As a consequence of ADHD, a lack of understanding of the seriousness of this condition, and the often cruel comments made to them, sufferers often compensate for the condition by self-medicating: abusing drugs and/or alcohol, or smoking heavily, or consuming large amounts of caffeinated beverages, all of which can cause other devastating, long-term health issues and are no replacement for proper treatment.

If you have ADHD, it certainly didn't appear out of nowhere. It's likely that you were undiagnosed as a child, and there's at least a 40 percent chance that one of your parents had ADHD (whether or not they were diagnosed).[4] However, just because the condition's roots are often in childhood and genetics play a role does not mean it has to be a life sentence.

How ADHD Affects You

I don't need to tell you that ADHD affects most aspects of your life—from work situations to interpersonal relationships. Over time, your self-esteem has been affected and the ways you interact with others attempt to compensate for, and conceal, your vulnerabilities. You realize that you aren't as productive as those around you and even simple things like household chores can throw you for a loop.

For those around you, your condition is challenging as well—especially before you have a diagnosis. People treat you differently, either because of your erratic behavior or because your actions have labeled you as unreliable.

Jen is a thirty-seven-year-old computer programmer who was diagnosed with ADHD about a year ago. She was energetic, highly engaging, and full of life when discussing her feelings about the potential utility of technology—she was a pleasure to speak with and the interview passed quickly. Jen complained of ongoing issues with task completion, time management, distractibility, restlessness, impulsive talking, boredom, and trouble waiting in spite of treatment.

Even though she had been diagnosed previously, my first step was to corroborate the diagnosis. Jen acknowledged the above symptoms of ADHD, which were affecting her both at work and at home. She was having difficulty holding down a job and had had several programming jobs in the last year. Jen indicated that she often got bored on the job and had difficulty adhering to her employer's schedule and time line for projects. She said that she always felt she worked better for herself. Jen felt most fulfilled when freelance writing about the Internet and technology issues. She was disorganized in completing tasks at home, worked longer hours than she needed to, and was somewhat socially isolated. Her symptoms of inattention, distractibility, difficulty completing tasks in the allotted time, impulsive talking out of turn, and interrupting others when busy dated back to early elementary school.

Jen noted a variety of personal and professional issues that had affected her in her adult life. At the peak of her writing career about eight years ago and before her ADHD was diagnosed, she overscheduled herself and took on too many projects. She was married at the time and working long hours trying to get her work done. In an attempt to increase her productivity she fell into regular cocaine use for a period of several months. In the end she didn't get her work

ADHD Can Touch Every Aspect of Your Life

Individuals with ADHD often find themselves impaired in various aspects of daily life. The following are some of the key areas commonly affected:

■ Academic and/or employment problems
  · People with ADHD are more likely to have repeated a grade in school.
  · They may underperform academically and in the workplace.
  · They tend to change jobs often.
  · They are less likely to have climbed to the top of the economic ladder.

■ Driving problems
  · People with ADHD are more likely to have motor vehicle accidents. Their accidents are also likely to be more severe.
  · Individuals with ADHD do more false braking (braking for no apparent safety reason) than people in the population at large. They also are cited for more moving violations.

■ Lifestyle choices: heavy smoking and coffee drinking
  · They are twice as likely to smoke as people who do not have ADHD, and more inclined to consume caffeine.

> · They are at an increased risk of substance abuse if
>   not treated.
>
> ■ Problems maintaining relationships
>   · People with ADHD have higher rates of divorce and
>   separation than the public at large.
>   · They are more likely to experience marital stress.

done, and she lost her job and her marriage. At that time she slipped into a serious depression. She stopped the cocaine as she tried to right her professional and personal life and has not used it since. Jen then found work in computer programming. The work was steady and more structured than freelance writing, but she felt it was not stimulating enough and has moved between several jobs over the last couple of years.

Jen's story teaches us several important lessons about adult ADHD. Her major depression and substance abuse are common co-conditions that can accompany ADHD in adults. It appeared that she was self-medicating her ADHD with cocaine, which had serious consequences as it contributed to the loss of her marriage and her job. However, once Jen treated her ADHD, she did not use substances again.

There May Be More of You Out There

As you're reading this, you may wonder how I can say that eight million adults in this country have ADHD but only 15 percent of them have been diagnosed. If there are documented case histories for only 1.2 million people with adult ADHD, how can I state that there are 6.8 million more? Isn't that a little speculative?

Many factors must be taken into consideration. First of all, even if an individual is bothered by symptoms, they may not be enough to drive him or her to the doctor, because the individual may not draw a clear connection between symptoms and illness. People don't just show up for an annual exam and say something like, "Well, as long as you're doing my yearly blood tests and so on, why don't you test me for ADHD." In fact, patients often don't bring "ordinary" problems of daily life to their doctor's attention. They'll tell him about a recurring stomach problem but not that they (or their children) are getting bad grades in school. While there are all kinds of reasons for poor grades, most wouldn't think of mentioning it (or other "ordinary" problems that would be concurrently in evidence in an individual with ADHD) to their physician.

Then there is the fact that so many people with ADHD never even go to the doctor. Like all of us who plan those twice-yearly teeth cleanings and struggle to get there, the person with ADHD might back-burner a trip to the doctor, because they'll have to step off their treadmill to go—and they might not feel it's worth the effort. Also, we should factor in the reality of rising health care costs that keep people from seeking medical care, managed care that can limit the doctor-patient relationship, as well as the fact that men don't visit doctors as often as women, so there's less likelihood for the ADHD to be diagnosed.

For those who actually make it to the doctor, ADHD may not be recognized and addressed if the patient did not go in solely for those symptoms and if the doctor does not immediately recognize them. In fact, a recent study revealed that more than 40 percent of the undiagnosed adult ADHD patients had seen a health professional at least once in the past year without getting a diag-nosis.[3]

You May Not Know That You Have It

It is estimated that 85 percent of the eight million adults in our country with adult ADHD *are unaware* that they have it, and the 15 percent who know have probably only found out in the last ten years. This doesn't mean that the condition suddenly sprouted up like a new virus or an unforeseen consequence of modern living. Rather, it has been around for a long time, undiagnosed and with-out a name. What has changed the picture in recent years in rela-tion to ADHD is science's ability to probe the human brain with noninvasive techniques such as magnetic resonance imaging and positron-emission tomography (PET) in order to map the brain's structure as never before. Technicians can safely draw samples of bodily fluids and we now have machines that can analyze them with great accuracy. Using scanning techniques, we can watch a portion of the body as it functions electrically or chemically. Computers can process miles of data—sort it, compare, contrast, and evaluate it—to uncover crucial facts that may be buried in the pile of information.

Little by little, the data that shows the grouping of symptoms that accompany certain neurological facts has been gathered and examined. Explanations that connect causes with effects have been suggested, tested for reliability, and confirmed. Because of this, ADHD is now accepted as a diagnosable medical condition—and, in turn, it is becoming less socially stigmatized. Now that we know more about it, we are creating tools that help us view confusing and seemingly conflicting symptom profiles to better identify in-

The Economic Impact of Adult ADHD

Not only is adult ADHD frustrating to individuals and their families but it also takes a toll on the American economy. In fact, it is arguably one of the costliest medical conditions in the United States today. Consider these facts:

- U.S. household income losses due to ADHD total nearly $77 billion each year, according to a large-scale survey.
- More than eight million adult Americans, or 4.3 percent of working-age adults, struggle with ADHD.
- The average loss of household income per adult with ADHD ranges from $8,900 to $15,400 per year.[5]

dividuals with ADHD. The process is not over by any means, but as our knowledge increases, so too does our ability to identify the condition.

A Complex Diagnosis

Adult ADHD doesn't manifest in exactly the same way in every individual, which leads to misdiagnosis. While ADHD is grossly underdiagnosed, a great deal of self-diagnosis occurs, and about two-thirds of those who diagnose themselves with ADHD do not have the condition. So, how do you know if your symptoms are truly those of ADHD? A diagnostic tool called the DSM-IV has become particularly helpful in making a diagnosis. The DSM-IV details criteria for making diagnoses in neuropsychiatric disorders, including mood disorders (bipolar disorder, major depression, anxiety disorders). We will discuss the DSM-IV and its practical application later in this book.

DSM-IV Criteria for ADHD

I. Either A or B:

A Six or more of the following symptoms of inattention have been present for at least 6 months to a point that is disruptive and inappropriate for developmental level:

INATTENTION

1 Does not give close attention to details or makes careless mistakes in schoolwork, work, or other activities.

2 Has trouble keeping attention on tasks or play activities.

3 Does not seem to listen when spoken to directly.

4 Does not follow instructions and fails to finish schoolwork, chores, or duties in the workplace (not due to oppositional behavior or failure to understand instructions).

5 Has trouble organizing activities.

6 Avoids, dislikes, or doesn't want to do things that take a lot of mental effort for a long period of time (such as schoolwork or homework).

7 Loses things needed for tasks and activities (e.g., toys, school assignments, pencils, books, or tools).

8 Is easily distracted.

9 Is forgetful in daily activities.

B Six or more of the following symptoms of hyperactivity-impulsivity have been present for at least 6 months to an extent that is disruptive and inappropriate for developmental level:

HYPERACTIVITY

1 Fidgets with hands or feet or squirms in seat.

2 Gets up from seat when remaining in seat is expected.

3 Runs about or climbs when and where it is not appropriate (adolescents or adults may feel very restless).

4 Has trouble playing or enjoying leisure activities quietly.

5 Is "on the go" or often acts as if "driven by a motor."

6 Talks excessively.

IMPULSIVITY

1 Blurts out answers before questions have been finished.

2 Has trouble waiting one's turn.

3 Interrupts or intrudes on others (e.g., butts into conversations or games).

II. Some symptoms that cause impairment were present before age 7 years.

III. Some impairment from the symptoms is present in two or more settings (e.g., at school/work and at home).

IV. There must be clear evidence of significant impairment in social, school, or work functioning.

V. The symptoms do not happen only during the course of a Pervasive Developmental Disorder, Schizophrenia, or other Psychotic Disorder. The symptoms are not better accounted for by another mental disorder (e.g., Mood Disorder, Anxiety Disorder, Dissociative Disorder, or a Personality Disorder).[6]

Symptoms of ADHD are wide-ranging and can vary from chronic forgetfulness to criminal behaviors. This can make it difficult for a primary care physician to make a diagnosis and is the reason so many refer patients to a psychiatrist like myself who has a battery of tests to better determine the correct diagnosis. Add to that the fact that ADHD is not well known to the general public and that primary care physicians report a discomfort in treating it, and you have a complex issue indeed.

Tackling adult ADHD is a process that can yield great success when you team with a professional who understands the disease. Doing so can break the cycle within a family and prevent suffering. Generally, if a person doesn't manifest another extreme co-condition or hasn't fallen into self-destructive behaviors such as alcohol or drug use, ADHD can be treated while you continue to go to work and/or school. Medication and behavioral therapies can be administered with little interference in your regular routine, as well as counseling or coaching, which can be integral for long-term success.

The Three Subtypes of Adult ADHD

There are three distinct subtypes of ADHD, which are defined by the predominance of symptoms exhibited by the patient:

- inattentive
- hyperactive/impulsive
- combined (hyperactive/inattentive)

The combined subtype is the most common form and afflicts more than 70 percent of adult ADHD sufferers. The hyperactive/impulsive subtype is the least common and associated with less than 5 percent of ADHD sufferers. The purely inattentive subtype constitutes about 20 percent of sufferers. Despite the differing presentation of the symptoms (inattentive vs. hyperactive), the origin of the disorder is the same.

What You Can Do If You Believe ADHD Is Affecting Your Life

The first thing you must do is get an accurate diagnosis, which will also rule out any other health conditions. Not every physician is comfortable diagnosing ADHD, so it's important to see someone who has experience with the condition. Your primary care physician may have an understanding of ADHD and experience treating it. If not, he or she will refer you to an expert for a diagnosis.

Diagnosing ADHD, whether in adults or children, is a multi-step process. Often, when meeting a patient for the first time, I give them the ASRS-v1.1 Screener (Figure 1.1). This World Health Organization (WHO) screening test, developed by a work group of experts in adult ADHD, including doctors at Harvard Medical School, Massachusetts General Hospital, and New York University, identifies individuals at risk for ADHD. The screener does not give a full diagnosis but is a good first indicator of whether or not you have ADHD. Ninety-three percent of the individuals who screen positive turn out to have the disorder. The ASRS v1.1 Screener is readily available free of charge in several locations on the Web— including the WHO Web site and the Web site for the Adult ADHD Program at the NYU School of Medicine (http://www.med.nyu .edu/psych/public/). Please see pages 105–07 for a longer version.

During the diagnosis, we also screen for other conditions that may have symptoms that look like ADHD, or co-conditions that are often experienced alongside ADHD. It's important to rule out a battery of mental illnesses because, while their symptoms may be similar, the treatments can be very different and the medications can yield very different side effects.

Figure 1.1 ASRS-v1.1 Screener

I. INATTENTION

	NEVER	RARELY	SOMETIMES	OFTEN	VERY OFTEN
How often do you have trouble wrapping up the fine details of a project, once the challenging parts have been done?	0	1	2*	3*	4*
How often do you have difficulty getting things in order when you have to do a task that requires organization?	0	1	2*	3*	4*
How often do you have problems remembering appointments or obligations?	0	1	2*	3*	4*
When you have a task that requires a lot of thought, how often do you avoid or delay getting started?	0	1	2	3*	4*

II. HYPERACTIVITY-IMPULSIVITY

How often do you fidget or squirm with your hands or your feet when you have to sit down for a long time?	0	1	2	3*	4*
How often do you feel overly active and compelled to do things, like you were driven by a motor?	0	1	2	3*	4*

ASRS-v1.1 Screener copyright © 2003 World Health Organization (WHO). Reprinted with permission of WHO. All rights reserved.

Asterisk (*) indicates significant symptoms.

The good news is that ADHD is not a death sentence or even a life-threatening condition. In fact, getting a diagnosis is a good thing. Having a diagnosis gives you the luxury of a new beginning: Putting a name to the condition means that you can address it and create the kind of life you want, and know, you deserve.

How Adult ADHD Is Treated

There are several accepted protocols for treating ADHD, each supported by solid scientific studies published in medical journals. Today, many physicians and other practitioners also use and support the treatment plan we have outlined, some of them urged on by the studies, others by the success stories. In addition to publishing, my colleagues and I have spoken to many gatherings of physicians and psychiatrists eager to learn how to manage ADHD in their adult patients, and have conducted training programs. Treatment is life-changing for those afflicted and their family and friends. Time and time again, with the appropriate treatment plan, I've seen patients reclaim their lives.

When Tim, whom we mentioned earlier, was treated for ADHD and co-occurring conditions over a period of several months, he reported for the first time that he "felt better." He no longer interrupted me during our meetings and was able to hold down a job that he found unfulfilling while he looked for better employment. He eventually succeeded in finding more rewarding work and moved in with his girlfriend.

ADHD is treated with one or more of a combination of medications and complementary treatments, which I'll discuss in more detail in later chapters. The short-term goal of medication is to help the patient find some sense of stability. Over time, the medication is adjusted as necessary for daily use and the other treatment modalities are integrated into the overall plan.

New Frontiers

The early onset of ADHD in childhood suggests that the disorder might be associated with an early disruption of neural circuitry. Current magnetic resonance imaging (MRI) studies of the brain can help us to better understand which regions of the brain are involved in ADHD and how it affects cognitive functioning.

Other studies have unequivocally demonstrated that there is abnormal glucose metabolism occurring in the brains of adults with ADHD since childhood, which we'll discuss in more detail in chapter 4. Glucose is the body's primary "food" for the brain, and its metabolism refers to how it is converted into energy for fuel. A reduction in glucose metabolism indicates dysfunction. Studies of people with ADHD have shown that the most affected areas in the brain are the premotor cortex, cerebellum, and superior frontal cortex—areas involved in the control of attention and motor activity. Damage to these frontal lobes has been positively associated with impaired executive function. Excessive motor activity has been associated with damage in the basal ganglia.[7]

Because the human brain continues to grow and develop into adulthood, scientists hope to chart anatomical brain development in ADHD children and link it to cognitive changes in a normally developing brain. These comparisons may provide insight into the pathogenesis of ADHD. At this point in time these tests are not able to detect differences at the individual patient level and are not useful in the clinical evaluation of whether or not a patient has ADHD—they are research tools. Nothing currently replaces sitting down with your doctor and providing him or her with a comprehensive history.

What I've Learned

There are safe and effective ways of treating ADHD. I have seen my patients' lives completely turn around and individuals who others had dismissed as "flaky" and "unreliable" become productive persons with a better quality of life.

As many as 50 percent of people with ADHD have another condition, which complicates matters, most commonly depression, anxiety disorders, learning disabilities, or bipolar disorder. Finding a balance with this other condition, which we call a "comorbidity," is the true challenge and why non-drug treatments alone don't have much success.

During the many years I've been treating ADHD, I've learned about the many facets of this condition through both scientific study and observation of patients. My patients have been generous in sharing their symptoms and challenges, as well as their triumphs. I've learned so much from them and each year that passes shows me just how complex it is and helps me comprehend just how frustrating and infuriating it can be.

This book is the result of many years of hands-on treatment and research. I've treated thousands of patients who have traveled from just down the street to halfway around the world to find a solution for this devastating illness. With treatment, symptoms begin to disappear completely in most patients and they can begin to discover a new life with minimal side effects. This is not to say that recovery occurs immediately. It is necessary not only to find the appropriate medication and dosage but also to participate in other facets of treatment as well.

My intention in this book is to encourage you to find the truth about your condition. I'll help you determine if you truly have ADHD and what to do about it. You may very well have a co-condition, as mentioned above, that will factor into your treatment. But there is hope. In my field, we commonly treat patients with complex neurological and mental issues with great results. It's not always simple, but it's easier than living a life of chaos and uncertainty. You'll have some obstacles to overcome, but the information in this book will give you a springboard to your destination—renewed health.

In these pages you'll find a treatment that is appropriate for your situation. Partnering with your physician or psychiatrist is the first step in a successful treatment plan. You will have good days and bad days. Some will feel great and you'll be on top of the world. Others will reveal realities you've been incapable of acknowledging or dealing with, and addressing them will be challenging and may stir up emotional pain. But with time, and some of the coping skills I discuss, you'll notice that there are more good days than bad. You'll actually begin to go with the flow, instead of dropping into the abyss. Perhaps the most rewarding part of treatment is that it allows you to reconnect with family, friends, and loved ones and hopefully you'll rediscover a life full of the energy and happiness that may have eluded you. By following a treatment protocol, and partnering with your doctor, this is attainable. You'll see.

CHAPTER TWO

Not Just a Kids' Disorder:
How ADHD Affects Adults

Before picking up this book or being encouraged to read it, had you ever heard of attention deficit disorder or attention deficit hyperactivity disorder? Of course you did. What is the first thing that comes to mind when you hear the term ADHD? If your response is something along the lines of "That's something kids have," you are not alone.

Here are a few responses from some people we asked:

". . . those kids playing ball in the aisles of the supermarket."

"Joey down the street who can't read very well, but can build a pretty accurate model of the space shuttle out of Legos."

"That disruptive kid in my child's class!"

"The cute little girl in my daughter's class who gets so caught up in her daydreams that she forgets to go outside for recess."

"When I was a kid, they called them 'hyper.' "

People think of ADHD as a children's disorder for several reasons. The first is that the condition does occur and has its roots in childhood and is frequently mentioned in relation to a youngster's performance in school or adjustment to the classroom or home environment; in fact, that's probably how you heard of it. The second reason is that the medical profession first began examining the set of symptoms for a condition that was called attention deficit disorder (ADD) to diagnose and help children who were having problems adjusting to everyday life. (In fact, ADHD was called many things prior to ADD, including minimal brain dysfunction, which reveals our previous lack of understanding of the disorder.)

For quite a while, ADD was thought of as something that existed solely in childhood. Since parents, educators, and caregivers needed help working with children who were hyperactive and impulsive and not functioning at the level of their peers in both academic and social situations, that's where the energies of doctors and researchers were being directed.

Not Just for Kids

It wasn't until the mid-1970s that it was recognized that ADHD could persist into adulthood. As we've learned more about this disorder and treated increasing numbers of adults, we now know that as many as two-thirds of children with ADHD grow up to be adults with ADHD.

Making the transition into adulthood involves a great deal of change, and most people learn to cope with their evolving life as best they can. Although, on close scrutiny, an adult may be seen as uncommonly restless, he no longer climbs on his desk, bangs every new object he encounters, yells out whenever he has the urge, or manifests his inquietude as overtly as children might. The very symptoms that in childhood would have made his predicament so clearly visible to anyone around him are now things he has learned to manage—somewhat. While he may in fact still be restless, and still put himself in some kind of motion all the time, his everyday behavior may not call out "ADHD" with the same force that children's behavior does—although it still exists. Often, the frank hyperactivity of childhood is now felt as a sense of internal restlessness and discomfort.

Though real, physical (neurological) differences may hinder him in many aspects of daily living, the reasons for his difficulties may not be so obvious to him or those around him. Issues of time management and cognitive load that were managed so well by parents, teachers, and caregivers in childhood now need to be handled by the adult with ADHD, and are often done so badly. And even if the adult was diagnosed and treated as a child, he or she was in no way prepared for the rigors of adult life. So, as children become adults, the inattentive symptoms that were always present become more noticeable and troublesome—to themselves and to others.

Highly functioning adults with ADHD may be able to put on a good face, but that doesn't mean that things are okay. A person with ADHD may encounter problems in everyday life and not distinguish the challenges from the obstacles peers face in their personal lives or careers. Untreated, the condition becomes increasingly frustrating because he won't understand what is holding him back and sabotaging his every move. He may be passed over for promotions or is the first to be "laid off" when a company is restructuring. Often, he feels excessively faulted by others, and then blames himself as if he is deliberately refusing to make appropriate efforts. It may not occur to him or others that the barriers in his path are neurological in origin, nor will he know where to go to seek well-being.

When Francisco was recruited by the advertising agency, everything was looking up. He was bright and had great creative ideas. But then his life started interfering. He arrived late for client meetings and missed deadlines and progress reports. Clients complained, but the company liked him. The creative director kept giving him pep talks and promising him a great future with the company, if he could just "get it together." But he couldn't.

What Is ADHD, Really?

ADHD is a condition that exists not only in children but also, as we are now aware, in many adults. What is it and what causes it? Why do some people have it while others don't? And are there ways to predict who might have it and to treat them before the condition creates obstacles in their lives and pulls them down? We will explore the answers to these questions in this chapter.

What's Going on in Your Brain?

ADHD has its origins in the brain and is biological in nature. While those of us who are rational would say that any biological imbalance should be treated as such and not stigmatized, people with ADHD and other conditions that make them appear to be "spacey"

> Attention deficit hyperactivity disorder (ADHD) was first attributed to adults in the 1970s, more than seventy years after ADHD was first identified in children.

or not trying hard enough are unfortunately often treated as though it were somehow their fault. Trust me, it is not.

Persons with ADHD *are* treated differently than if they had high blood pressure or were in a wheelchair. It is a "silent" disability, as individuals with ADHD do not "look" different from others. Their behavior is attributed to laziness, selfishness, or bad karma, and people assume that they have brought it on themselves. And this is the tragedy that they live with every day, layered on top of their suffering from the disorder itself.

The brain is a very specialized living machine and as such has some characteristics in common with man-made devices, including simple ones such as matches and pushcarts and more complex and specialized ones such as lamps, water purifiers, computers, and cars. It has many complex parts that fit together in a way that enables it to work well. Like the rest of your body, it truly is a miracle of nature. It has electrical and chemical components. When all the components are working together harmoniously, the brain functions optimally. But because it is such a complex machine, a problem in one area may have adverse effects on the functioning of other parts. While a hammer with a dented handle can still be used to drive in nails or a lamp whose base has been bent out of shape may still be capable of supporting the wires that convey current up-to the light bulb—damage just one chip in a computer and the train of connections that enables it to work according to plan is disrupted. It might continue to do well on some tasks and then

Neuron (n.): a cell that transmits nerve impulses and is the basic functional unit of the nervous system.

suddenly bomb out when connecting what it has done to a final task for an expected result. That's what happens in the brain with ADHD.

Think of It This Way . . .

Let's imagine the brain as a dormitory, with lots of workers and messengers living in it, laid out so that everyone can function optimally. It has halls and stairways that allow the messengers to move from one area to another. Then, imagine what would happen if they moved into a house whose kitchen lay at the end of a hallway that was so narrow at one point that no one could get past it. If they wanted to go from the dining room, at the front of the house, to the kitchen, at the end of the hallway, they couldn't go directly from dining room to hallway to kitchen. Instead, they would have to go outside and climb through the kitchen window, or go all the way around to the back of the house and through the laundry room to get to the kitchen. Wouldn't it be easier for them to function in a house that was laid out more efficiently?

Obviously it would be. As it is, they'd probably stop using the dining room as a place for eating and eat in the kitchen instead. And even if the kitchen was too small, they'd squeeze themselves and the dining table and chairs in, trying to fit too many related activities into a space that wasn't laid out for them. That cluttered solution was the best they could do under the circumstances, even though it meant that the kitchen had to exist in a state of constant disarray.

Because of that disorder, they might not be able to prepare meals well, which would affect their health. The house might look like a regular house from the outside, but whether people knew it or not, no one living there would be able to function as easily as people whose homes weren't strategically blocked on the inside. The owner of that brain would get the best its workers could produce in the unfavorable conditions they were working in, but would probably accomplish less than someone whose brain functioned effectively.

Or imagine a car whose engine runs so slowly that in order to perform well some of its parts have to compensate by constantly kicking and cranking. You might think this frantic activity was excessive but in fact all that extra motion is compensation for a poorly constructed motor.

Too Much Stimulation, or Not Enough?

One of the reasons adult ADHD isn't easily identified is because the *hyperactivity* element seems to ease in adulthood. Therefore the standard "itchy bottom" syndrome that many young children manifest in school (which is so readily associated with ADHD) isn't present in many adults. But while it may not be overtly obvious, it is still present.

One interesting fact that research has uncovered is that the hyperactivity seen in many persons affected by ADHD is *not* the result of an excessively active brain. Rather it is often a brain so sluggish in certain aspects of its functioning that it activates the body as a way of bringing itself up to the lowest threshold of activity needed to function. So, the brain of that child running around wildly (or the adult whose feet are constantly jiggling) is not putting him in such a spin because it is out of control, but rather because their internal throttle on impulse control is not working well,

Did You Know . . . ?

ADHD is an actual health condition, not a behavioral problem. Experts refer to it as a *neurobiological* disorder. Individuals with ADHD have lower levels of two chemicals, norepinephrine and dopamine, in the areas of the brain that have been shown to affect attention and impulse control, specifically the area just below the front of the brain, as we'll discuss in more detail in chapter 4.

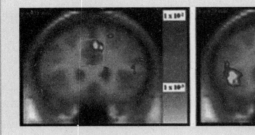

NORMAL CONTROL   ADHD

ADHD Adult vs. Normal Controls (fMRI During Perceptual Task)*
ADHD brain fails to utilize normal pathway to process data
*Stroop task utilized
MGH-NIMR Center & Harvard-MIT CITP, G. Bush et al., *Biological Psychiatry.* 1999 June 15;45(12):1542–52.

The diagram above shows what occurs in the brain of an individual with ADHD when performing an attention-demanding task. Notice the use of accessory and less efficient pathways instead of those in the prefrontal cortex, where normal brain function occurs.

It's a lot like driving a stick-shift car up a steep hill. The car will only power forward of its own volition to a certain level of RPMs. Then you have to manually shift gears and the car may

> stall or rear back. The driver then presses on the gas to move
> forward. It works, of course, but it's not the most efficient way
> to get there.

so the so-called "normal" window between thought and action
has shrunk.

This, of course, answers the question of why a child or adult who
appears overstimulated is given a medication in the stimulant class,
such as Ritalin (methylphenidate), Concerta (extended-release
OROS methylphenidate), Focalin XR (extended-release d-methylphenidate), Adderall XR (extended-release mixed amphetamine
salts), or Adderall (mixed amphetamine salts). Stimulant medications such as Ritalin Concerta and Adderall and non-stimulants
such as Strattera (atomoxetine) can give a measure of calm and
composure to hyperactive individuals with ADHD. They stimulate
the release of neurochemicals just enough to let the brain operate
properly from within without having to kick itself into activity
from without.

What Happens with Children Also Affects Adults

As we discussed in chapter 1, there are four cornerstones of diagnosing ADHD: (1) sufficient inattentive and/or hyperactive-
impulsive symptoms; (2) impairment (trouble) from the symptoms;
(3) childhood onset; and (4) the symptoms are of ADHD and not
of another disorder. Evaluating these symptoms and getting a correct diagnosis is the first step in treating the illness.

Evaluating ADHD

The presence of more than a handful of the following symptoms indicates that an individual may have ADHD. We'll go into more detail in chapter 5, but note that eighteen symptom categories for ADHD are listed below. Individuals need to exhibit a sufficient number of symptoms as part of making the diagnosis.

Inattentive Symptoms

- Fail to give close attention to details or make careless mistakes at work.
- Have difficulty sustaining attention in tasks or fun activities.
- Don't listen when spoken to directly.
- Don't follow through on instructions and fail to finish work.
- Have difficulty organizing tasks and activities.
- Avoid, dislike, or are reluctant to engage in work that requires sustained mental effort.
- Lose things necessary for tasks and activities.
- Easily distracted.
- Forgetful in daily duties.

Hyperactive Symptoms

- Fidget with hands or feet or squirm in seat.
- Leave seat in situations where seating is expected.
- Feel restless.
- Have difficulty engaging in leisure activities quietly.

- Feel "on the go" or "driven by a motor."
- Talk excessively.
- Blurt out answers before questions have been completed.
- Have difficulty waiting turn (impatient).
- Interrupt or intrude on others.[1]

Without getting into the technicalities of the brain anomalies in an individual with ADHD, let's look at some of the behaviors found in individuals with this condition. Let's first look at the behaviors we also see in children, because they provide clues to what eventually develops as the child grows up. We find *inattention*, which manifests as apparent carelessness in doing work, the seeming inability to listen when spoken to directly, not following through on or finishing tasks, and difficulty organizing tasks. The avoidance of tasks that require sustained mental effort, the habit of losing needed things, distractibility, and forgetfulness are some characteristics of inattention.

The ADHD child also exhibits *hyperactivity;* he or she squirms and fidgets, can't seem to sit still, and frequently gets up when staying seated is required. He runs about and climbs, appears unable to participate in "quiet" activities, talks excessively, and, at times, appears almost motor driven. *Impulsivity* is also in evidence. The child can't wait his turn, answers questions before they've been fully stated, and interrupts activities.

Furthermore, some of these symptoms will have been present before the age of seven and will have made it harder for the child to adjust to the routine in at least two settings (home, school, or social settings). There will be clear evidence of significant impairment in social or academic settings and the symptoms are not ones that show up only during the course of another disorder or could be better accounted for by another mental disorder. Sound familiar? Basically the same thing happens in adults, but adults can often create mechanisms, or a framework to deal with it.

Another manifestation that is problematic and stigmatizing for adults is underperformance—especially in the workplace. It's frustrating for the individual because her supervisor may assume that she is performing at her best, and that her best is just not very good. If she knows she could do better and should be able to achieve more, it adds additional stressors that exacerbate the situation. Underperformance is considered another form of impairment in ADHD. Not doing what you are capable of doing can have a significant impact on one's life and is one of those easy-to-miss symptoms as the individual at first blush might be perceived as functioning and holding down a job, etc.

As I mentioned before, adults have learned how to cope with and manage society's demands to the best of their abilities. As an ADHD child gets older, he learns how to control the most blatant forms of hyperactive and impulsive behavior—largely due to peer pressure. He doesn't blurt out everything that runs through his head, or run around with such abandon. Though to the clinical eye hyperactive or impulsive characteristics may still exist in adults diagnosed with ADHD, these traits are not as visible as they are in elementary school-age children, and therefore ADHD in its adult form may not be as noticeable as it is in children.

The amount of things adults need to think about and manage on a daily basis is much greater than that of an elementary school-age child, and should be considered. Let's highlight the higher level of organization and planning required in adulthood: Adults with

ADHD have the "full" days that we all do—they need to get up in the morning, get their children (who often have ADHD) off to school, go to work and work a full day, help with homework, put dinner on the table, put the kids to bed, pay the bills, go to bed themselves, and then do it all over again the next day. As adults we've gone from being managed by others in childhood to not only managing ourselves but managing others. And this is hard enough for the healthy individual.

ADHD, however, is not usually a condition that lingers for a while and just disappears. At least two-thirds of children with ADHD carry it on into adulthood, and the jury is still out on the others. So don't dismiss it: ADHD is *not* a childhood disease. It is a condition that is the result of brain differences that do not go away with age. It is, therefore, a condition that may persevere over a lifetime, and the individual who is afflicted must be treated and learn to adapt to utilizing treatment and life skills that may be very different from their friends and colleagues.

Now You See It, Then You Didn't

Most adults who learn that they have ADHD will, upon careful examination of their childhood problems and behavior, discover that they had ADHD in childhood as well. We use the term *presentation* as in "there can be adult presentation of ADHD" to describe the situation in which the symptoms of the disorder become clearly problematic in adulthood and, subsequently, the individual is diagnosed for the first time. *Presentation*, however, is not *onset*. There is no such thing as adult-onset ADHD; the roots of the disorder lie in childhood. It may not have been diagnosed, but the symptoms were present.

It has been estimated that 4 percent of adults in the United States, or about eight million people, have attention deficit hyperactivity disorder. (If this percentage held worldwide, it would translate into 240 million people!) Of these U.S. estimates, it is believed that 80 percent do not know they have the disease or are untreated. These numbers are considerably higher than for children, for whom we do a much better job of recognizing the disorder and getting them into treatment. In fact, a recent Centers for Disease Control (CDC) survey found that 8 percent of school-age children had been diagnosed with ADHD, and of these almost all had received treatment. However, a recent report shows dismal numbers in adults: Only 1 percent of adults in a prescription database were being treated for adult ADHD, which indicates that the condition is undertreated as 4.4 percent of the adult U.S. population has ADHD.

Something Else to Blame Your Parents For

And if those statistics aren't shocking enough, it has also been found that the disorder is inherited, or passed on through the genes. In fact, the heritability of the disorder is an amazingly high 80 percent, which means that if someone has a relative with ADHD, there's a significant likelihood that that person is also carrying the genes for it. In adult presentation of ADHD, the genes were always there but did not begin to express the traits until childhood was over. We'll talk more about the causes of ADHD in the next chapter.

How are all those adults with undiagnosed ADHD getting by? We can assume that they are managing in one way or another, but they are probably not doing as well as their peers who don't suffer from the condition, or as well as they could be doing had they been diagnosed and treated. And let's not forget the central point: *ADHD is a neuropsychiatric condition that arises because of structural and functional abnormalities in the brain.* They're not lazy. They're not arrogant. Simply put, people with ADHD have brains that are built a little differently and work a little differently.

We also must factor in the quick pace of today's society. Current adult life is conducted rapidly in today's information age, with a large volume of material and skills to master—much of which is at our fingertips and has to be handled quickly. The obstacles that many of us hurdle day to day bring out the symptoms in a person with ADHD, which further complicates their lives. While we like to call this information-heavy society ADHD, the actual disorder is not a by-product of modern life. Tools that were supposed to make our lives easier, such as the Internet, have conversely put us into a constant multitasking mode. In order to navigate this busy world, the person with ADHD must approach life and its tasks differently.

This difference, of course, manifests in behavior and abilities. Although someone with ADHD might appear lazy or ambivalent to someone who reads their behavior in terms of what she knows about her own behavior and motives, it's not that individuals with ADHD aren't trying and just *won't* do things exactly as others do. The truth is that without availing themselves of the help that is out there, they can't.

Facing the Obstacles of ADHD

Because of their unique brain wiring and chemistry, adults with ADHD may have difficulty doing tasks that require vigilance, organization, planning, complex problem solving, verbal learning, and memory. In other words, they have a hard time functioning as successfully as others at work and, quite possibly, at home as well.

As children they could usually rely on the adults in their lives to manage certain things for them, but when they become adults the burden of management falls on them and they can't just jump in and take on those tasks.

It is crucial, especially in our contemporary high-stakes society, that we be able to plan, evaluate, and follow through on directives or adapt to changing circumstances. Management requires attentive skills and it is these very skills that prove especially difficult for individuals with ADHD. They may be trying hard but still not performing as well as others. Though they do whatever they can to cope with difficult situations, their solutions may not be effective. The resulting underperformance pushes them further into a corner. They find it difficult to climb the socioeconomic ladder or hold on to the same job. It's harder to get professional work. Marital difficulties escalate and often end up in separation or divorce. Even a simple task like driving a car becomes a challenge: They have unusually high numbers of speeding violations, collisions, and accidents. They may have resorted to substance abuse and/or display psychiatric disorders of one kind or another.

ADHD individuals may appear not to be working hard when, in fact, they are running at full throttle inside. Those differences in brain structure and chemistry may mean that, figuratively speaking, they have to run though enormous inner mazes in order to come out a few steps ahead or simply to tread water. Think about this in terms of doing a task and you will see that in the time that someone with normal brain function can cover many steps, someone with ADHD may get ahead by only a few. So when you look at only the tangible results of a day's work, the individual with ADHD has underperformed compared with his colleagues. In fact, in adult ADHD, that is the factor that drives the person to seek a diagnosis.

Getting to Work

Since we are under constant scrutiny in the workplace, and how much we produce becomes the most important measure of our success, someone who is producing less than his coworkers is going to encounter problems. Because ADHD is not visible from the outside, its effects are not taken into consideration by employers or managers. Its symptoms are those that everyone displays occasionally, but others can control. It's not so simple for the individual with ADHD.

Bob is a thirty-one-year-old engineer/designer who presented for evaluation of adult ADHD, as both his sister and father were recently diagnosed with the condition. He described lifelong issues with inattention, easy distraction, difficulty prioritizing and organizing, needing deadlines to complete work and often taking longer to complete tasks than the time allotted, forgetfulness, daydreaming, and frequently losing things. These symptoms went back to elementary school and led to his not doing as well in school as he felt he was capable of (and what his teachers thought he was capable of too). He liked to be busy and worked long hours, supplementing his work with adjunct teaching at a local college. He denied any significant hyperactive-impulsive symptoms. After discussion of that he was correct and that he had ADHD, inattentive subtype, we discussed treatment options and agreed on a trial of the stimulant, sustained-release OROS methylphenidate (Concerta). He did note significant improvement in his attention, distractibility, and procrastination while on Concerta 54 mg/day. However, he felt that his symptoms returned in the early evening and that he was jittery if he took an additional dose of short-acting methylphenidate in the afternoon to extend the duration of the medication. As a family member had recently had a positive response to the non-stimulant atomoxetine (Strattera), Bob expressed a desire to try switching to this medication. We cross-tapered his Concerta over to Strattera by lowering his Concerta and increasing the Strattera on a weekly basis. He felt significant improvement throughout the day and into the evening when he was on Strattera for about a month at a dose of 75 mg/day. He is now better able to work late and has just started a new job with increased responsibilities.

Coping with ADHD in the Workplace

The reality is that, with or without ADHD, most of us have to work. With ADHD, productive, fulfilling work can be extremely difficult. Be aware that you may have some options and/or protection under federal law. However, the decision to reveal to your employer that you have ADHD is a personal one, and you should discuss the implications with your mental health professional.

Americans with Disabilities Act (ADA)

ADHD is covered under the Americans with Disabilities Act and certain individuals with ADHD may be entitled to receive special work accommodations to assist with their needs.

Just because you've been diagnosed with ADHD doesn't mean that you'll get these accommodations, however. You and your employer or supervisor will be the best judges of that. However, if you require assistance to perform your job, you are protected under the ADA. But be careful about demanding your rights. Much like the right-of-way in traffic, if you are inflexible in your demands, you can create bad interactions.

Keep in mind that you may have to educate your employer about your condition. If you've been able to successfully hide your symptoms on the job, your employer may not be aware that you've experienced challenges above and beyond the norm in the workplace. This would make it harder to make your case, even though your needs may be great.

Consider your needs carefully before requesting accommodations and be reasonable and flexible. You may want to consult with your doctor to determine what has worked well for his or her other patients. Be fair and keep in mind that your employer is trying to run a business and may be willing to help you perform your job better, but must balance your needs with the needs of all the staff. ADHD is an explanation, not an excuse.

Become adept at explaining your symptoms and how they affect your work performance. Try not to make excuses, and offer solutions. For example, if everyone in the department takes turns picking up afternoon coffee at the shop down the street and you stress for hours before and after your turn—and still mess it up—ask for a pass on it. This may be a small example, but one you shouldn't skip over.

Or, if you've been asked to compile a competitive analysis for your company, and the final product will be a daunting 190 pages in eight sections, see if you can split the project with someone or complete it in sections. Be creative. Your employer will recognize your enthusiasm and work ethic and try to find ways to assist you.

Possible Accommodations in the Workplace

Once you have been diagnosed with ADHD, schedule a time to meet with your employers or supervisor to discuss your situation. Most employers are happy to work with you to modify your work environment, provided it is not overly expensive or complicated.

Facilitate Job Focus

- Provide a tape recorder for meetings.
- Modify training materials to include audio or video tapes.
- Allow use of "white noise" at your desk, or headphones to reduce distractions.
- Set up room dividers to lessen distractions.
- Provide a quiet workplace that limits distractions or a private office.

Assist with Deadlines and Organization

- Create flexible work schedules or reduce work to part-time schedule.
- Restructure deadlines.
- Allow projects to be completed in sections, when possible.
- Assist with organizational skill development.
- Color-code materials, such as filing systems, using different colored papers for important memos or coding each project with a certain color.
- Restructure files or workspace to create a more even flow

of work, as well as to reduce steps to completion
of work.

- Reassign job duties.

Provide Time- and Job-Management Tools

- Software, timers, alarm clocks
- Organizational helpers such as day planners, PDAs
- Computers
- Spell-check and grammar-check software

Special Considerations for Women with ADHD

When we discuss ADHD, it is often described in terms of men's symptoms. But women suffer as well, and often longer because their symptoms are not always as obvious as men's. It isn't that ADHD only describes men's symptoms—it is that ADHD was originally conceived as a disorder primarily of hyperactive boys. Women have a higher burden of inattentive symptoms and often are not diagnosed until adulthood, at which time they are diagnosed almost equally with men (in children, we identify the fidgety/disruptive symptoms more than the inattentive ones).

Okay, So What Do You Do?

For people who believe their lives have been made difficult by adult ADHD, seeking help and obtaining a diagnosis is a very important first step, but it is only the first step. ADHD is a complex condition with many variants. Almost everyone with adult ADHD can obtain help that will enable him or her to function more successfully and happily in the world, but this can only be done after the problem has been identified. The longer the condition persists undetected, the more problems will pile up in that individual's life, problems whose consequences will have to be dealt with. Again, obtaining an early diagnosis is the first step toward successful living.

The good news is that ADHD can be treated, and every day your options increase and your chances for living a full and balanced life improve. There's no magic bullet for ADHD, or even a tidy little treatment that works equally well for all individuals. But there are effective treatments that, when taken under the supervision of a trained medical professional, can help you begin the process of reclaiming your mental health. The ASRS v1.1 screening test mentioned in the previous chapter and explained further in chapter 5 gives you more insight into what symptoms indicate a need for a more formal diagnosis.

Remember, many people respond dramatically to medication and experience life-changing alterations in how they function after taking them. Others benefit from a combination of modalities, such as coaching and cognitive behavioral therapy, and finding the right medication and dosage. These complementary therapies teach them how to apply appropriate responses and solutions to different situations and help them work out coping strategies to deal successfully with the challenges of everyday life. If you approach treatment as a multifaceted process, like petals on a flower, you'll soon see that the combination of individual therapies and solutions has the potential to create a solid, whole you.

Adult life demands self-management, which requires good attentive skills, and adult ADHD, which impairs those very skills, makes it harder for people to succeed in relationships, in jobs, and in some activities, such as driving, that are essential for modern-day life.

If an adult has ADHD, it is not, first and foremost, a *problem*. It is a *reality*. Working with the fact to prevent its becoming a problem is the most positive approach one can take. We will explore it further in later chapters.

CHAPTER THREE

Red Herrings and Red Flags: What ADHD *Isn't*—and Where It Might Be Hiding Behind Other Symptoms and Coping Mechanisms

Barbara was avoiding washing the dishes—a task she did not enjoy at all—by reading a magazine, when she came upon an article about ADHD, a condition she knew virtually nothing about. It was actually the illustrations accompanying the story that first caught her eye, and she began by browsing through the article, becoming more and more interested as she read on. By the time she reached a list of symptoms she had slowed down and was reading with care and attention. She read about distractibility and getting sidelined, restlessness, disorganization, and having trouble starting or finishing tasks.

By the time she finished the article, she was pacing around her sloppy house thinking to herself, "Oh my God, I've got ADHD!" She was so worried about it that she put off washing the dishes for yet another hour. But then she glanced at the clock and realized that her mother, who was a neatnik, would be arriving with her critical eye in thirty minutes, so she buckled down and got to work. Barbara finished the dishes and tidied the house with amazing efficiency, and even managed to find time to run a comb through her hair and change her clothes.

Barbara did *not* and does not have ADHD, even though she identified with all the symptoms in the article. Many tendencies or behaviors exhibited by people with ADHD also appear in people without it, and the manifestation of one or another of these traits or behaviors is not unusual. In fact, almost everyone on the face of the earth, at one time or another, has exhibited most of the behaviors on the list. However, it is the total picture of these states and actions—their intertwined existences, intensities, and frequencies—that delineate ADHD. In the composite situation described above, Barbara had to deal with the results of certain choices she had made in her day (she chose not to wash the dishes earlier and had a messy kitchen), but she was not held back from being able to do things later. She may not have felt like doing anything at noon, but once she determined it was absolutely necessary, she could, and did, wash the dishes and tidy her house. That's the rub: Someone with ADHD will try and fail, although the task seems perfectly within reach. So it's not an easy diagnosis. The determining factor is whether or not these symptoms have been more or less present throughout that person's life and have caused *real* problems in two realms of that person's life. As illustrated, Barbara was not impaired by the traits that caused her to put off doing some tasks for a while.

For example, Michael, a busy twenty-six-year-old CPA, is always losing his keys—and his BlackBerry, his wallet, and the security card to his office building. When he gets home from work, he tries to remember to empty his pockets on the table by the front door, but somehow it doesn't happen. His girlfriend keeps threatening to get him a "man purse" for all his stuff, but then jokes that he'd probably misplace that, too. These chronic bouts of losing things, and the inevitable frustration that follows, may appear symptomatic of ADHD, but in Michael's case there's no impairment, which means he doesn't have ADHD—despite his annoying symptoms. A colleague of Michael's had his own problems. Recently, Jed found himself in the emergency room on a Saturday night after a fender bender coming home from an afternoon barbecue. He was so shaken by the event that he visited his therapist a few days later because he thought his recent driving problems might be related to a psychological or health condition and he was afraid. The psychologist asked Jed a few directed questions and came up with a diagnosis of acute stress and alcohol abuse: Jed had just opened a restaurant and was under a great deal of pressure to perform—not only in a demanding restaurant environment, but for all the investors (including his grandmother!) who had put in tens of thousands of dollars. When he did have time off, he tended to spend it "blowing off steam," i.e., drinking. He also drank with the bar customers at his restaurant and, of course, who can turn down a free drink happy diners send their way? But Jed's situation was a bit different: He had a family history of excessive alcohol use and he met a few other criteria that persuaded the therapist that he should seek help for his condition before it became a problem. But Jed does not have ADHD, either, although his symptoms mimic that of a person with ADHD and a comorbid disorder, which we'll discuss in more detail later.

So, How Can You Tell Whether It's ADHD or Something Else?

Many people wonder about ADHD or suspect that they, or someone they know, might have it, but they do not have the expertise to diagnose it—even though many of us think otherwise.

There are several indicators to determine whether or not a person has ADHD. First of all, the disorder doesn't come out of nowhere. While the symptoms may worsen, or become exaggerated, they were ever-present. So, if there's no childhood history of symptoms and the symptoms seemed to have come "out of the blue," it's unlikely that the person has ADHD.

ADHD is a disease that includes multiple impairing symptoms—not just attentional ones—that are often context-based and can be influenced by whether or not there were significant stressors present, or by task difficulty. An analogy often used from child ADHD is that the school reports significant inattention, trouble with task completion, daydreaming, and hyperactivity, and the child's parents resist an evaluation because the child can play video games for extended periods of time.[1]

If an individual is experiencing symptoms that suggest he may have the condition, he should initiate the process of diagnosis by speaking to a professional, possibly the family doctor, who may refer him to a psychiatrist or psychologist. (We'll discuss the full process of diagnosis in chapter 5.) While the family doctor may not feel comfortable making a definitive diagnosis of ADHD, he or she may be familiar with the ASRS v1.1 Screener often used to make an early determination. Based on an early consultation, your primary care physician (PCP) would likely be able to reassure an individual such as Barbara that the totality of her symptoms do not point to

ADHD, and may be comfortable making a diagnosis in another patient. In other cases, a PCP may be more comfortable referring the patient to the people and places that can provide the most inclusive help, such as a psychologist or a psychiatrist.

Most of us have learned that whenever we have troubles in life, other troubles also arise. Let's say your car breaks down en route to work and you don't arrive on time. Your supervisor is fastidious about being on time, and the initial mishap, a transportation malfunction, means your name is added to the list of people who were late. Other problems may follow. You may rush through work to make up for the time you missed and do something incorrectly. You may skip lunch in order to catch up and then, instead of eating something on the fly, you make due with too many cups of black coffee and end up with both an upset stomach and a strong case of the jitters. So one malfunction may bring a whole train of other ones in its wake. We've all been there and know how frustrating running on a treadmill—expending energy without getting anywhere—is. Multiply that many times and you have ADHD every day.

Common Co-conditions

Co-conditions (or "comorbidities," as they're technically called) are the rule rather than the exception with ADHD. It is estimated that 50 to 70 percent of adults with ADHD have another mental health disorder.[2]

As the table on page 64 indicates, there are several conditions that adults with ADHD commonly struggle with. These include abuse or dependence on drugs or alcohol, anxiety and mood disorders (including depression, bipolar disorder, and dysthymia),

Comorbid Psychiatric Disturbances Are Common in Adults with ADHD

Antisocial Disorder (10%)

Major Depressive Disorder (35%)

Bipolar Disorder (15%)

Anxiety Disorders (40%)

Substance Abuse Disorders (50%)

Shekim WO et al. *Compr. Psychiatry.* 1990;31:416–25.
Biederman J et al. *Am J Psychiatry.* 1993;f50;1792–98.
Wilens TE, Faraone SV, Biederman J, *JAMA.* 2004 Aug 4;292(5):619–23.

and certain learning disabilities. In other words, if you have adult ADHD, there is *an increased likelihood* that you may have one or more of the other conditions that are often associated with it. Some of these co-conditions manifest similar symptoms as ADHD, which can make diagnosis challenging—and why you should not self-diagnose. Some of the other conditions can safely be managed concurrently with ADHD. Others need to be addressed and successfully treated and managed before the ADHD can be treated. The pros and cons of the treatment hierarchy is something that a skilled medical doctor will be able to explain to you and help you with.

Max, forty-eight, came to me after several months of increasing depression. He was seriously depressed, with suicidal thoughts, and unable to function in his job as a litigation attorney at a law firm. He was experiencing interrupted sleep, ruminative (recurrent) thoughts of his failings and problems in his marriage, decreased appetite, and diminished sex drive. He was referred by his gastroenterologist, who felt that the stress of his depression was exacerbating his ulcerative colitis. Max related that he had done little work in high school, but attended a prestigious college and law school.

At the time of his initial visit, I diagnosed Max as having a major depression, and treatment with psychotherapy and antidepressants was initiated. Over several years his depression at best partially responded to a variety of antidepressants, including several serotonin reuptake inhibitors (SSRIs), and he found it increasingly difficult to work. His depression responded best to a combination of bupropion (Wellbutrin) and an SSRI.

Max described his thought processes as "clearer" when taking Wellbutrin, which led me to reexamine his history of attentional issues. Although he had originally indicated that there were no attentional issues at home or school, upon review it became apparent that he chronically procrastinated, beginning as far back as elementary school. This was never an issue for him in secondary school or college because he was so bright, but it did present problems in law school, where he had difficulty getting the work done to the best of his abilities when he left it for the last minute.

In Max's work as a practicing attorney, some issues had arisen prior to the onset of his depression about his procrastinating, talking out of turn with and not listening to partners, and prioritizing his work. His wife complained that he didn't listen, didn't see things through, and didn't get things done around the house. One intervening factor was that although Max could remember issues about his school experience, it was difficult to obtain a clear history about his early family life as his home life had been rather chaotic and unstructured. Additionally, his father was deceased and he rarely spoke to his mother. However, he was able to get some information from his aunt, who told him, "Of course, you were always on the move and climbing on things," and that adults would use terms such as "whirling dervish" to describe him as a young child. Few things held his attention for long periods of time and he often moved from one thing to the next. They thought little of this, as he was so bright and engaging.

It became apparent that Max had ADHD in addition to a serious major depression. One tip-off was his report of improved focus while taking Wellbutrin, which does have efficacy in ADHD. It was difficult to take a childhood history because of the severity of his depression and the chaotic nature of his upbringing. However, when more information and a more complete picture came to light, the diagnosis of ADHD became clear—and Max received a treatment plan that has helped him dramatically improve the quality of his life.

Looking for ADHD When Other Conditions Are Diagnosed First

Because ADHD commonly occurs along with other conditions, it is important for individuals with mood disorders, anxiety disorders, and substance abuse problems to be evaluated for ADHD. It is not uncommon for individuals with mood or substance abuse disorders not to improve in spite of multiple medication or psychotherapy trials because their ADHD was missed.

Since comorbidities are so common, the most pressing disorder should be treated first. If there is active substance abuse, then it is not possible to treat the ADHD until the substance abuse is brought under the treatment umbrella. If there is a major depression or bipolar disorder, given the severity of the symptoms of those episodic disorders, it might be prudent to treat them before the ADHD, which is more or less lifelong. If the comorbid disor-

ADHD Comorbidity in Adults with Other Psychiatric Disorders

Disorder	ADHD Rate
Major Depression[1]	20%
Bipolar Disorder[2]	15%
Generalized Anxiety Disorders[3]	20%
Substance Abuse[4]	25%

▶ **Re-evaluate *refractory* patients for ADHD**

1. Alpert et al. Psychiatry Res. 1996.
2. Nierenberg et al. APA Presentation, 2002.
3. Fones et al., *J Affective Dis*; 2000
4. Wilens. *Psych Clin N Am*; 2004.

der is more chronic, such as with anxiety disorders or chronic depression, the ADHD is more commonly treated first and the other disorders treated second if they persist (as some of the symptoms might improve with amelioration of the ADHD).

Having ADHD doesn't guarantee you a bout with a secondary or tertiary condition, but it does mean you have a greatly increased chance of it. For the best possible treatment outcome and, eventually, your desired quality of life, it's important to get a complete diagnosis that encompasses any and all related conditions so they can be addressed and treated.

Co-conditions Often Found in People with ADHD

It's important to take a look at some of the problems that are often encountered when looking at the lives of people with ADHD.

Remember, these conditions are *not* ADHD, but they often come along for the ride and complicate the picture. The situation can be further complicated by the fact that people who have one of these other conditions *without having ADHD* are sometimes misdiagnosed as having ADHD. The problem with such mislabeling is that even if the symptoms are alike, the conditions' neurological origins are very different and medication(s) that may be effective in helping people with ADHD may be very harmful for a person misdiagnosed with another condition. Some conditions that may coexist with ADHD but are *not,* in themselves, ADHD are:

Bipolar (Manic-depressive) Disorder

In this disorder people undergo dramatic mood swings, called "episodes" because they last for a week or longer. Up to 20 percent of persons with ADHD may also have bipolar disorder. In the manic phase, a person has a period of extremely elevated moods, which can include excessive talking, giddiness, and an overwhelming feeling of infallibility. He cannot sleep and goes to extremes in what he does. This is the "motor driven" phase of the disorder. The downside of this phase is clinical depression. Each of these phases can last days or weeks, and there may be periods of normal mood between episodes.

Depression

Almost 35 percent of adults with ADHD also have depression, be it a significant episodic major depression or dysthymia. Typically, ADHD occurs first and depression occurs later as a comorbidity. Adults with depression often become withdrawn, lose interest and/or pleasure in the things they used to enjoy, experience insomnia or can't get out of bed, lose their appetite, and think or talk about dying. Researchers also debate whether a percentage of the chronic depression that is comorbid with ADHD may be a consequence of the years of frustration, poor self-esteem, and impaired social/occupational functioning if the individual has lived with untreated ADHD. It is believed that both environment and genetics play a part in depressive illness. Current studies suggest that both ADHD and depression share a common underlying genetic link, since families with ADHD also seem to have more members with depression than would be expected by chance.[3]

Anxiety Disorders

Up to 30 percent of children and 25 to 40 percent of adults with ADHD will also have an anxiety disorder. The anxiety disorders that comorbidly affect individuals with ADHD include generalized anxiety disorder, panic disorder, social phobias, obsessive-compulsive disorder, and post-traumatic stress disorder (PTSD). Patients with generalized anxiety disorder chronically worry excessively about a number of things (school, work, etc.) that are beyond normal everyday worries, have difficulty dismissing these worries, may feel edgy, stressed out, tired, or tense, and have trouble getting restful sleep. Patients with panic disorder have brief episodes of severe anxiety (panic attacks) that intensify over about ten minutes with complaints of pounding heart, sweating, shaking, choking, difficulty breathing, nausea or stomach pain, dizziness, and fears of going crazy or dying. These episodes may occur for no reason, and sometimes awaken patients. Patients suffering from social anxiety disorder or social phobias have fears of performing routine acts in public/observed situations, such as speaking, eating or meeting new people. This can lead to social isolation and avoidance, which can complicate the social impairment seen in adult ADHD. Obsessive-compulsive disorder is characterized by recurrent intrusive thoughts (obsessions), and compulsions (repetitive acts that the patient finds difficult to control, such as checking behaviors or hand washing). You may recall the Jack Nicholson character in *As Good As It Gets* as a classic example of someone with obsessive-compulsive disorder.

Patients with PTSD have been exposed to a significant trauma, such as a murder, robbery, or a life-threatening situation and they experience recurrent thoughts about this situation, which they find difficult to control. They are also likely to reexperience the traumatic incident when exposed to stimuli reminiscent of the event. The difficulty concentrating, hypervigilance, and easy startle seen in patients with PTSD can be similar to ADHD symptoms. PTSD and untreated ADHD patients are also at higher risk for substance use and dependence. When evaluating individuals with possible PTSD and ADHD it is critical to take a longitudinal history, as the PTSD symptoms have an onset after the traumatic incident, while ADHD symptoms do not have such a precipitant.[4] Genetic research suggests that ADHD and anxiety are separate disorders and are likely inherited independently of each other.[5]

Oppositional and Conduct Disorders

About 40 percent of individuals with ADHD have oppositional defiant disorder. Oppositional disorders encompass a variety of defiant and negative behavior. When the behavior is more extreme, at times dangerous, and involves aggression, it is said to be the result of a conduct disorder. Conduct disorder occurs in 20 to 25 percent of adults with ADHD. CD states are characterized by defiance, disobedience, and hostility. The classic bad boy may, in fact, be someone whose behavior is created by the condition rather than someone who chooses to be "bad." Conduct disorder, if unaddressed, is thought to be a precursor to antisocial personality disorder (sociopathy). Antisocial personality disorder is comorbid with ADHD (mostly in patients with untreated ADHD). In fact, several surveys have found high rates of untreated ADHD in prison populations.

Substance Use Disorders

Substance issues are of big concern when diagnosing ADHD because more than half of individuals with untreated ADHD in adulthood will develop a substance abuse disorder in their lifetime.[6] The substances of abuse include alcohol, marijuana, and cocaine (the latter has effects on norepinephrine and dopamine—the chemicals thought to be primarily involved in ADHD as discussed in more detail in chapter 4), but can be expanded to include extreme caffeine and tobacco intake.

Adults with ADHD have elevated rates of smoking and report particular difficulty quitting. A recent survey from Massachusetts General Hospital found that adults with ADHD are twice as likely to smoke cigarettes.[7] In another study young adults with ADHD were found to have much higher odds of smoking regularly, and the number of ADHD symptoms reported correlated with an increased risk of smoking regularly.[8]

Additionally, researchers at Massachusetts General Hospital have found an increased risk of substance abuse in untreated adolescents with ADHD as compared to a group of adolescents receiving treatment for their ADHD. This data supports the concept that some of the substance abuse seen in adolescents and adults may be the result of attempts to self-medicate ADHD.

What to Do If You Have One
of the Co-conditions

"Basic" ADHD *is* often complicated by other psycho-neurological conditions, such as mood disorders and bipolar disorders. Discovering the totality is important because you can't paint an accurate picture of a person's condition without adding everything in, nor will a treatment that does not consider the whole be as effective as one that does. Yet it is important to know which things that are impacting a person's life are the results of ADHD, and which are riding alongside.

Again, the most important step is to get a comprehensive diagnosis because at least one "auxiliary" state exists in 50 percent of people with ADHD. Clearly that will cloud or complicate the principal condition and require treatment in conjunction with the treatment for ADHD. The *order* of treatment will depend upon the relative severity of each condition. As you can see, diagnosis can become complicated and, because of this, identifying all the factors involved in each individual case can often be done with much greater accuracy and assurance by appropriate agencies or specialists who focus on neuropsychiatric maladies. Knowing all this, as described above, a family doctor may ask some patients to seek the advice of experts in the field. Far from wanting to wash his hands of them, he wants to be sure that they get the most appropriate care.

Clearly, a high level of diagnostic sophistication is called for. When looking for and at coexisting mental health conditions, it is important to determine which ones are actually present, and then to identify the most prominent and impairing disorder so it can be treated first. Of course, the other conditions still need to be treated, but that will be done sequentially.

The long-term history is key in treatment. If a patient has a long history of substance use disorder, then of course that should be addressed first, because the longevity of the disorder often impacts its seriousness. There are exceptions in the case of bipolar conditions and debilitating depressions; all patients should be diagnosed and treated individually.

For example, if an adult exhibits a serious mood disorder—bipolar disorder of a manic type or a major depression with suicidal thoughts—the mood disorder *must* be addressed first. The mood disorder is separate from the ADHD. While the adult ADHD will be present throughout the patient's life, the mood disorder—which manifests in episodes, one of which is occurring at the time help is being sought—can be life-threatening. Clearly, the priority is to treat the most serious disorder first, then work on the other things that will affect the rest of his life. However, if the depression or anxiety disorder has been continuous and it is determined that it is less impairing than the ADHD, then treating ADHD first would be the most beneficial plan. Alcohol and substance abuse are of great concern when treating adult ADHD, and treatment will not be effective unless the person is actively participating in a treatment program.

Sometimes ADHD is discovered in the course of diagnosing one of the other conditions. Statistics show that individuals who have other neuropsychic disorders (such as mood disorders or substance use disorders) are also likely to have adult ADHD 15 to 25 percent of the time. This is reverse ADHD comorbidity. Doctors who are examining a patient because of a different diagnosis may end up diagnosing adult ADHD, too, even though ADHD is *not* the condition that was originally suspected.

The point of understanding these red flags and co-conditions is not to paint an even more dire picture for those who suffer from these disorders. Rather, it is to recognize the scope and nature of the problem—so that we can go about treating it and alleviating what's causing the problems in the first place.

CHAPTER FOUR

What Causes ADHD?
What We Know So Far

By now, you have learned enough about ADHD to know that its basis is mostly biological, with heredity contributing about 75 percent of the causal factors.[1] It isn't behavioral in the sense that someone with the condition *chooses* to behave, or not to behave, in specific ways. The physiological makeup of people with ADHD impels them to respond to certain situations in certain ways. Though the triggering structures are out of sight under their skulls, they are physically challenged in the same way as people with observable bodily differences, though of course their limitations tend to be expressed in outcomes that may appear to be chosen rather than done because they had no other recourse.

If a person whose left arm is much shorter than his right arm only reaches for things on a high shelf when they are positioned on his right side, we can see the reason for it and understand that if he refuses to face the other way when reaching up, he is doing this out of necessity rather than stubbornness, rebellion, and so on. A person with one leg markedly shorter than the other will not be able to run like most folks and may have great difficulty even walking.

A one-eyed man who is trying to carefully view a scene before him might turn his head back and forth more frequently than someone with vision in both eyes. Though most people can recognize that individuals with such physical disparities are making heroic efforts on an hourly basis just by performing tasks that would be labeled easy by an "ordinary" individual, it is not as simple to see that people with ADHD are doing this too because the source of their problems is hidden from view. Fortunately, our rapidly improving technology with its sophisticated tools and measuring instruments has enabled brain science to look inside the body to see causes of behavior that are hidden from the eye. As understanding advances, public awareness will follow.

Genetics Plays a Distinct Role

Happily, more and more people are now aware that ADHD is a "biological" fact that—along with other biological conditions such as having blue eyes, brown eyes, large breasts, small breasts, and so on—exists when a child comes into the world. All babies' eyes, for example, appear similar at birth, but each individual's eye color becomes clearly expressed in the months that follow. A girl does not grow breasts until puberty, but when she does, they are not large or small because of something she ate, or something someone said. She has been carrying around the genetic blueprint for their construction throughout her life, and when she reaches adolescence and it is time for her body to build them, it will follow the instructions coded into its master plan—a collection of genes that tell the body everything it will do and how and when they will be done during every stage of life.

Each cell in a person's body contains an identical packet of genes. If the cell is in an eye, the genes that affect eye function get busy while the ones that have to do with functions far removed are dormant. At the same time, the genes that are dormant in the eye cell may be working very hard in cells in another part of the body. Bodies are conglomerates of masses of cells acting and interacting with one another, and genes control each cell's behavior. Our genetic makeup is important in determining many aspects of our physical and behavioral existence.

A great deal is known about what the genes are (they are composed of DNA), how they are organized, and how they work, but for this discussion it is sufficient to say that a typical gene carries the instructions for making a protein molecule, and that thousands of different protein molecules, each specified by a different gene, are needed for each cell to build itself and to perform its many complex functions.

Most genes come in a number of slightly different forms, each of which leads to a slightly different version of the protein. Because there are thousands of human genes, most of which come in many slightly different forms, every human being, with the exception of identical twins, is unique. On the other hand, certain combinations of variants of a few genes can be responsible for a particular trait (for example ADHD), and so any individual with that combination will display the trait.

We inherit our genes from our parents. They are found in the long DNA molecules that lie inside the chromosomes in the nucleus of every cell. The chromosomes are found in pairs, and so, therefore, are the genes. Generally speaking, if Mom carries ten genes (five pairs) that are important for determining a certain trait, Dad will also carry ten genes for it. Almost every cell of our bodies will carry the same ten genes for that particular feature, half of which we got from Mom and half from Dad. The only cells that carry fewer genes (half the usual number, to be precise) are the reproductive cells, called gametes, which exist as eggs in women and sperm in men. These are the cells that unite at conception. As soon as a sperm fuses with an egg and deposits its complement of genetic material, the egg is fertilized. It now has the usual cell's amount of genes and is capable of dividing like other cells. But before the cell divides, each gene duplicates, and when division occurs one copy of each gene goes to each daughter cell. Each of those cells also divides, and so on and so on. After much growth and gradual changes among different cell groupings (which are becoming individualized in many ways but not in the genes they hold within) the cell groups differentiate into various organs and organ systems. Altogether, they form the body of a new baby with a combination of characteristics all his own.

In the lottery that determines the exact combination of genes that we get from each of our parents, special cells in our parents' bodies give rise to gametes (egg or sperm cells) by undergoing *meiosis,* an unusual type of cell division in which each daughter cell (called a gamete) receives only half of each type of genetic material contained in the parent cell. Remember those ten eye color genes each parent has? Each gamete will get five —which five being determined by chance. But the wheel of fortune has not stopped spinning yet. There are plenty of sperm cells carrying different combinations (only five per gamete, remember?) of Dad's ten original eye color genes. Which one will end up fertilizing the egg? It's a dance of chance, a bit of a lottery that determines the exact combination of traits an individual ends up with—the reason why every child is unique.

Some of the results of the gene mix may be clearly visible when

Baby is young, while the effects caused by other genes may not be so quickly visible because they won't affect immediate development but will be expressed at a later stage. Someone may have inherited his mom's small ears and his dad's brown eyes and tendency toward baldness (this last fact won't become evident for a long time). Baby Jim, for example, carries a gene for blue eyes that came from his mom, and one for brown eyes from Dad. Because the brown gene is dominant it will overpower the blue gene and Jim will have brown eyes. However, when Jim grows up and becomes a father himself, he can still pass on that blue-eye gene to his child. And if, when he does, that child's mother is blue-eyed, with only blue-eye genes to pass on to her offspring, Jim may end up with a blue-eyed son or daughter. When more dominant genes overrule other genes, it doesn't mean that they cease to exist. They are still there in all the cells, including the ones that divide to become gametes, and can possibly be passed on to the next generation. This is as true of genes that contribute to ADHD as it is for ones that determine eye color.

Upon investigation, it can be found that, although certain symptoms were not taken as indicators of ADHD during their youth, most patients with adult ADHD *presented* those symptoms consistently since early childhood. Why were those behaviors there? Did the individual just "choose" to be that way, or did he act in manners that had been genetically coded in? Clearly, something more concrete than "choice" was in operation.

Bodies (brains are very much a part of these) are formed in the womb, under the direction of the genes carried in each cell of the developing person. They were present in the fertilized egg that grew into a ball of cells and from that into an embryo, a fetus, a newborn baby, a toddler, a five-year-old, and so on. That person continued developing according to the same genetic map it carried in the womb. The genes (and they are present in every cell) *heavily influence* a person's life at each stage of maturation, sometimes because they have caused body structures to be built in a particular way, sometimes because they are *not* acting, and often because they are initiating, or orchestrating, chains of events that affect bodily function. Notice that I said "heavily influence" instead of "determine" here because I'm a doctor talking about ADHD in a medical context that has management of and relief from problematic symptoms as the desired outcome. Our science is progressing, and as it does, we are finding strategies and treatments that, by also influencing an individual, can counteract some forces that create problems. It is also true that we are increasingly viewing ADHD as a condition that comes into being when a *number* of influences (genetic influences being just one) are present at the same time.

The genes (and we have identified some of them) that, in combination with one another, create the condition we call ADHD are handed down from generation to generation. If a parent has ADHD, each of the genes that created the condition in that parent has a chance to be passed on to the offspring. Does that mean that the child will have ADHD? Not necessarily, since his biological makeup will depend on which genes he gets from both parents and the combination may not cause the condition in him. Does it mean that a child of a parent with ADHD is more likely to inherit the condition? Yes. If both parents have ADHD, is the child even more likely to have it too? Yes again. Does it mean that the offspring of an ADHD parent who doesn't have ADHD might grow up and have a child with ADHD? It's possible. Someone who clearly had ADHD as a child but seems to be in remission as an adult might similarly carry the genes, although there is some evidence to suggest that, in some cases, genetic factors were not the primary cause of those cases of childhood ADHD. A family history of the disease is an indicator that other family members, whether diagnosed or not, might be carrying some of the genes that, in combination with other genes, produce ADHD. Looking backward, does it mean that a parent whose child has ADHD has the condition himself though it's never been labeled? There's certainly a possibility of this. We now know that ADHD tends to run in families. If one member has it, some of his relatives may too.

Non-genetic Causes of ADHD

Are there non-genetic factors that can increase the likelihood of a child being born with ADHD? Do things other than heredity bring about those particular structural differences in the brain that create ADHD? This appears to be the case. Substances introduced into a mother's body during pregnancy can alter cells in the fetus. They may be introduced through ingestion. A mother who smokes or uses drugs or alcohol during pregnancy may be putting her unborn child at risk of ADHD. Evidence for this is mounting. Anything that changes the normal chemical environment in which the fetus is developing (including maternal malnutrition) may affect the very regions of the developing child's brain that are implicated in ADHD. It also seems that the poor health of the pregnant mother, or delivery complications involving toxicity, can have negative influences on a fetus—with ADHD as a possible outcome.

Since you now know that ADHD is a disease that arises through a number of factors—one of which is heredity—that cause the brains of people with the condition to function a little differently, you are probably asking yourself the next question: What is different in the form or function of the brains of people with ADHD? What actually happens there that brings about the behavior and state of being that we usually find in ADHD individuals?

Before we get into the specifics of actual brains, let's look at an analogy that may help us get the big idea. Imagine that a construction team gets together to build a new high school, working from plans they have been given. They are very good followers who obey instructions to the letter. Each workman frames the area he has been directed to construct, doing the very best job he can with the materials that have been provided. Other workmen, equally conscientious, follow, installing pipes, electric cables, and so on. Walls are built and painted. Equipment is moved in. Each workman follows the instructions he has received.

Now imagine the new school building. It has large, well-equipped classrooms, an amply stocked library, a nice cafeteria, an auditorium, playing fields—everything. There is one problem, however. The hallways that connect all these rooms are so much narrower than hallways should be that it takes hours for the students just to get into the building.

If some of the classrooms had been constructed a little off plan it wouldn't have been so bad, but unfortunately there is virtual blockage of the hallways connecting all the rooms. The students have a new school that looks great from the outside, but they can hardly use it! Days there are full of problems. The pupils, who have been provided with many good things to use, want to work hard but they can't! The whole place is dysfunctional. When the bell rings and students need to change classes, the halls are impassable. Makeshift alternatives develop. Students can be observed using ladders and climbing in and out of windows to get to their classes. People observing from afar think they are just a bunch of rowdies when that is not the reason they are behaving so unusually. Unfortunately, it takes so much time and effort just getting from place to place that there is little left for learning.

This example should certainly not be taken literally, but I hope it serves to show how genetics matter. If we consider genes as the blueprints, and every human body as a building, the instructions coded into those genes determine the state of the building. If there are flaws in the blueprints, the building will be flawed. And if the problems exist in places that are structurally or organizationally important, the whole building may be compromised. Someday, medical science may be able to *correct* the problematic instructions before construction begins, but until that time it can only assist the occupants of the building in navigating the flawed structure.

Studies have shown that a number of genes have been implicated in ADHD; no one gene is predominant, and the effect of each of these genes is modest at best. A list of genes possibly involved includes the Dopamine D4 receptor (DRD4); Dopamine D5 receptor (DRD5); Dopamine transporter gene (SLC6A3); Dopamine Beta Hydroxylase (DBH); Synaptosomal-associated protein of 25 kDa (SNAP25), a variant of the Serotonin transporter gene (SLC6A4); and the Serotonin 1B receptor (HTR1B). There is little overlap of these genes on specific chromosome regions, indicating "genes with moderately large effects are unlikely to exist."[2] Therefore, genetic testing to examine individuals at risk for ADHD is not likely to yield positive results with our current level of understanding and has no clinical usefulness at this time.

I have used a building as a symbol for the human body, but, as you know, a human being is much more complex. The human body can't be torn down and reconstructed. It may be possible to make modifications, but the main "structure" has to be accepted as is.

Now the focus shifts. Though the question of *why* an individual was born with ADHD should be asked, other important questions are: What parts of this structure don't work as well as they should in combination with other parts? What can we do to make the whole thing function as well as possible? What can we do to help the person living in this body?

Let's look at what scientists found out about the brains of people with ADHD that sets them apart from the population at large. Before we do that, however, we need to review what we know about the brain.

The brain is a large, complicated, and multifaceted organ that serves as the body's control center. It sits at the top of your head, protected by the hard bony skull that encloses it, working unceasingly. You can study the brain for your whole life and not know a fraction of all that we have learned about it. You can think of it as a living network of computers, as a city that acts like the capital of a country, as a control and communications center. But it is an amazingly complex set of cells.

The brain is comprised of many areas that serve different functions. Each area is connected to all the other areas. An amazing amount of communication and feedback is constantly taking place from region to region. Some areas are connection centers, relaying the messages constantly streaming in from all parts of the body to other centers of the brain, or relaying instructions to the various body systems.

As would be true in a supercomputer, parts of the brain are constantly receiving messages from other parts of the body and from within itself, comparing or contrasting them, reacting to the results of those activities by producing other information, and then possibly relaying that all over the place for feedback and fine-tuning before coming up with a response, perhaps a set of precise instructions it will send to the body, which will carry them out through actions. A computer might send something to a printer, or store it within its own memory; a brain might instruct an arm to write a sentence while storing the content of the sentence in memory. While the computer might stop at this point, the brain never does. It will be busy receiving input about the state of the body and the consequences of its last actions from other parts of the body, retrieving information from memory to store alongside new facts, sorting out the information and sending it on to the appropriate sites within, and so forth. A seemingly simple action may involve millions of chemical/electrical signals and thousands of information pathways, as signals pass between networks of *neurons*, along the whole map of the brain. If one area can't keep up with the activity in another region, the computer might bomb out on the task, or the person be unable to function well in some aspect of his life.

Over years of research, we have built up a substantial body of evidence that links certain structural and chemical irregularities in the brain with specific problems that go hand in hand with ADHD. Abnormally low levels of dopamine and norepinephrine, two important neurotransmitters that affect areas of the brain that enable a person to pay attention to and maintain interest in an ongoing activity, seem to be involved in both the cause and the perpetuation of ADHD. The frontal cortices, cerebellums, and subcortical areas of the brains of individuals with ADHD have less volume than the corresponding areas in people without the condition. Functional imaging studies (done by means of functional magnetic resonance imaging [fMRI]) of the brains of individuals with ADHD have also revealed that some important circuits, especially those involved in motor control, executive functions, and inhibition

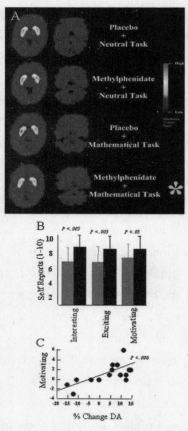

Nora D. Volkow, Gene-Jack Wang, Joanna S. Fowler, and Yu-Shin Ding. "Imaging the Effects of Methylphenidate on Brain Dopamine: New Model on Its Therapeutic Actions for Attention-Deficit/Hyperactivity Disorder." *Biological Psychiatry*. 2005 June 1;57(11):1410–15.

of behavior, are not performing as well as they should. These loops, which must provide feedback to the cerebral cortex if it is to adequately regulate behavior, function under the control of dopamine and norepinephrine, the very neurotransmitters that have been shown to be underactive in the brains of people with ADHD. When stimulants that block the action of chemicals known as dopamine transporters (by whisking dopamine away from a site) are administered to these individuals, they function better. There is some ev-

Patients with ADHD Have Neuroimaging Abnormalities

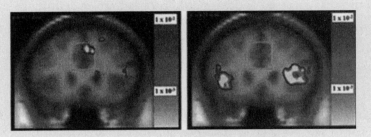

NORMAL CONTROL   ADHD

G. Bush, et al., *Biological Psychiatry.* 1999 Jun 15;45(12):1542–52.

The brain scans on this page and the previous page illustrate:

- global and regional glucose metabolism by PET scan reduced in adults who have been hyperactive since childhood.
- largest reductions in the premotor cortex and superior pre-fontal cortex.
- when presented with an interesting task, adults treated with methylphenidate show increases in dopamine.
- the anterior cingulated cognitive division (ACcd) plays a central role in attentional processing.
- during an attentional cognitive interference task (Stroop test), patients with ADHD failed to activate the ACcd, but instead activated a frontal striatal insular network.
- the defect is not produced by globally poor neuronal responsiveness.

idence that the dopamine transporter gene, which regulates the production of this chemical, is implicated in ADHD. Is dopamine unavailable to these individuals because their cells cannot produce an adequate supply, or is the problem the result of a slightly deviant gene, which directs cells to send in too much of a substance that transports a needed one away? While we cannot yet definitively explain *why* dopamine is not able to activate these brain regions of ADHD individuals as it should, it is clear that the chemical must be accessible if these areas of the brain are to do their job correctly. In time, we expect to understand this more fully.

Now we will take a moment to look at the *H*, hyperactivity, in ADHD. Most people assume that the excess motion exhibited by people with ADHD is the result of an overactive brain. Appearances can be misleading. As I have said, advances in technology have enabled us to look within the functioning brain. In the brains of some ADHD individuals, those who just can't stop bouncing around, we don't find corresponding cerebral activity. In fact, we find just the opposite: Cortical areas that should be lit up by the processes involved in normal functioning lie in the darkness of severe underactivity. When stimulants (drugs that, by immobilizing dopamine transporters, make dopamine more accessible to the cells) are administered, the underactive areas of the brain of many of these people begin to function more normally and the outward overactivity subsides. The same chemicals that drive ordinary people into a frenzy, calm the hyperactivity associated with ADHD because in this case they are not overstimulating a brain, just enabling it to use enough of the neurotransmitter needed to function normally!

The presumed location of the problem is in the prefontal cortex (the area below the front of the brain) as shown in the imaging data shown previously.

I hope you now have a better picture of the physical facts behind ADHD—the ones that cause people to have it in the first place
as well as the neurological events that produce actual symptoms in
an individual with the condition. Please remember that medical science still has much to learn. Right now a lot of work is being done
to answer questions and discover more about issues raised by the
many facts we have already uncovered. I don't want to imply that
we are working in the dark because we aren't. However, we are dealing with an organ so complex, and factors that include so many in-
terdependencies, that as our comprehension grows, our knowledge
horizon expands into the unknown, and we set out to learn more
about a host of things that may increase our understanding of the
physiology of the condition we call ADHD—and, in turn, our ability to alleviate it.

CHAPTER FIVE

Getting an
Accurate Diagnosis

Unlike many other disorders and illnesses, ADHD can be dif-ficult for clinical practitioners to diagnose. This is because there are no definitive biological indicators, such as elevated levels of glucose in the blood or urine, to suggest its presence. Patients report symptoms of inattention, easy distraction, restlessness, and organizational difficulties, along with behavioral patterns of interrupting others and fidgetiness. A positive diagnosis of adult ADHD is dependent upon a doctor's ability to recognize the symptoms, ascertain their severity and frequency, qualify the impact they have on the patient's life, and verify the childhood onset of symptoms through a series of interviews and evaluations.

Before I explain the diagnostic tools and procedures in detail, let's take a brief look at what too often goes wrong in diagnosing ADHD in adults—that is, the pitfalls both doctors and patients should strive to understand and overcome.

A Tricky Diagnosis

As adult ADHD has only recently been widely recognized and qualified as an adult disorder (see box, page 98), there remains limited reliable information for both clinicians and sufferers to adequately educate themselves about the disorder. Recent statistics suggest that 15 to 20 percent of people being treated for anxiety, depression, and substance abuse have been incorrectly diagnosed and may be suffering from adult ADHD.

What's more, the symptoms of adult ADHD are subtle, and shift over time and from situation to situation. Many of the symptoms are perfectly normal for individuals to experience at one time or another during the course of their lives, e.g., restlessness, procrastination, and inattentiveness due to external mitigating factors. To distinguish symptoms of ADHD from what are simply responses to life situations (and from medical conditions, most notably sleep disorders) requires that the doctor listen to the patient and put the symptoms into a "big picture."

Another stumbling block to getting an accurate diagnosis is that many clinicians may not be comfortable diagnosing a disorder that might call for the prescription of controlled substances, i.e., stimulants. Consequently, clinicians often refer patients to a specialist such as a psychiatrist. For some patients, this referral is stigmatized or frightening, and for others it proves too costly due to inadequate health care coverage.

Subtle Cognitive Behaviors

The range of expressions of ADHD symptoms in adults is broad. Examples include an overwhelming desire to be successful, leading to a compulsion to work, and not being able to relax on vacation.

Others with ADHD choose occupations that require constant energy output in the form of moving or talking (e.g., carpentry, sales, marketing), while some people work two jobs to keep themselves "busy." Common symptoms include frequently losing things such as cell phones and keys; poor planning, which leads to missed deadlines; and procrastination. Some ADHD sufferers can't finish projects, or have to have a project in progress at all times. And others self-medicate in socially acceptable ways such as drinking a lot of coffee and smoking a lot of cigarettes. Doctors need to get to know the patient and his history to be able to recognize these behaviors as symptoms of ADHD instead of just aberrant behaviors.

Symptoms That Evolve Over Time

As I've described earlier, ADHD has roots in childhood. However, many adults with the condition were not diagnosed as kids, and their symptoms lessened and changed over time. Hyperactive symptoms, the most obvious of all symptoms expressed in children, lessen at a much faster rate than inattentive symptoms, which can be confusing for clinicians who have little experience with the adult form of ADHD[1, 2]. The frank hyperactivity of childhood morphs into a sense of internal restlessness that is felt rather than manifested. Also, as we will discuss below, adults learn to cope with their symptoms and guard against manifesting the most stigmatizing aspects of the disorder. For example, running around and climbing on things is a symptom in the diagnostic criteria for childhood ADHD, whereas adults with ADHD feel restless but don't climb on top of their desk as this will not be well received in an office environment. Similarly, many ADHD adults exercise on a daily basis to appropriately discharge some of these restless feelings, or schedule bathroom breaks during a meeting that will require them to remain seated for a prolonged period of time. In the section below, we will look at some of these coping strategies and the ways they can interfere with an accurate diagnosis.

Paul is a thirty-seven-year-old psychologist who came to my office nine years ago for evaluation of possible ADHD. At that time, he was working as a computer programmer but had lost several jobs because of his difficulty in learning new material. He indicated that he was aware of difficulties in concentration and attention from a very early age.

Paul indicated that he never was a good reader and had difficulty remembering what he had read. He was a B+ student in elementary and middle school, but had obtained his bachelor's degree at a local college after running C's his freshman year at another university and withdrawing because of poor academic performance. He felt he was just skating by. His returning to college close to his parent's home was helpful in terms of his parents being able to provide some structure to his schoolwork. He took courses that required essay writing, since completing tests in a set amount of time was always problematic for him. He described that he needed to leave things for the last minute to marshal the energy and effort to complete them; this led to substantial anxiety as to whether the projects could be completed. He had always wanted to be a psychologist and teach, but did not know whether he could pass muster.

Paul had a history of chronic anxiety and worry and depression. The anxiety and dysphoria would often compromise his ability to interact with his peers and his school performance. At times when the anxiety peaked he would feel overwhelmed and have a fear of losing control, with increased heart rate and shortness of breath.

In our first visit Paul endorsed significant issues with inattention, easy distraction, trouble seeing things through, impulsive talking out of turn, misplacing items, talking a lot, interrupting others, drifting off and missing key parts of conversations, and procrastination. After reviewing his history, we discussed that I felt that Paul had ADHD, combined subtype, in addition to the comorbid disorders of a mixed anxiety disorder with features of generalized anxiety disorder and panic disorder and dysthymia (chronic depression). Prior to initiating treatment, we decided to obtain neuropsychological testing for educational reasons as Paul intended to attempt to apply to psychology graduate school programs. This psychological testing revealed Paul having an above average IQ of 116, but that his achievement tests revealed underperformance relative to his IQ. He had significant deficits in verbal attention, shifting sets, and processing speed.

We agreed to embark on a course of stimulant and anti-anxiety/antidepressant medications to treat his combined subtype ADHD and anxiety and dysthymia. He also agreed to initiate a course of cognitive behavioral therapy to help him manage these symptoms and plan for his day-to-day activities. His depression and anxiety were significantly improved with treatment with the antidepressant fluvoxamine nightly and clonazepam (a benzodiazepine antianxiety medication) to be taken as needed if panic anxiety occurred. His ADHD symptoms were substantially improved with the sustained-release stimulant OROS methylphenidate (Concerta) at a dose of 36 mg/day. However, he felt a need to extend the duration of effect of the Concerta as he needed to study into the evening, he additionally took short-acting dexmethylphenidate, also known as d-methylphenidate (Focalin), in the late afternoon.

Paul was able to enroll in and complete a master's program, which led him to feel that he was ready to apply to psychology graduate school. Paul was accepted and with accommodations of extended time for test taking and the ability to meet regularly with his advisor to plan his studies and thesis, he just received his Ph.D. He is now teaching at a local university and feels that he has finally fulfilled his dream. Paul indicated that the road to success required extra effort on his part and even though he was told by others that he would not be able to see it through, his perseverance/effort and ability to stick to the treatment plan of medication and CBT let him achieve his goal.

Coping Mechanisms

Adults who grew up without pharmacologic treatment for their ADHD invariably develop compensatory strategies in an attempt to minimize the expression of their symptoms and the impact they have on their day-to-day activities. These sometimes elaborate coping strategies often alleviate, or even eliminate, the impairment. If doctors are not looking for ADHD, they will not see it. If they don't ask patients about impairments and coping strategies, they are likely to miss the ADHD symptoms. For example, if an individual is dependent on a spouse for organizing him at home, and an executive assistant at work, he may not respond accurately to a general question about organizational difficulties. If the question brings to light his reliance on others for organization and planning, the full extent and impact of the adult ADHD symptoms can be ascertained, as there are obvious costs in having to rely on others in this way.

Furthermore, there are times when coping strategies in and of themselves can be impairing, and it is important to assess their impact during an evaluation. Let's look at Jen, a computer programmer in her thirties with combined type ADHD. When I first asked her about issues of misplacing items and easy boredom she indicated she did not have any problems as she was never bored and never misplaced anything. However, it turned out that it took her more than an hour each morning to find items that she needed, and that she always carried a bag of drawing and reading material in case she found herself with downtime during the day, as she always needed "something to do." The hour she lost in the morning collecting her things often made her late for appointments and significantly impaired her functioning. It was only by thorough questioning that her symptoms and coping strategies became apparent. There are sets of questions your doctor can use to thoroughly evaluate your adult symptoms, and we will discuss these later in this chapter.

The Importance of Seeing the Big Picture

A positive ADHD diagnosis can also be easily missed because interviews between doctor and patient tend to focus on the cross-sectional questioning and not on the past, such as examining what has happened in the patient's life in the last several days, rather than on lifelong symptoms. Also, patients may not exhibit symptoms in the one-on-one setting of a doctor's office. As discussed previously, symptoms tend to come out when individuals are doing things they find difficult or uninteresting—they are "context based," meaning their manifestation is based on the setting at hand. Often symptoms are minimized in individualized settings, which are inherently less distracting than group settings. Such could be the case in a doctor's office where a patient does not

ADHD Timeline

Since the early 1900s, when ADHD was first described, studies have been conducted to determine why seemingly normal children (and eventually, adults) could behave so poorly and suffer so greatly. Originally attributed to brain dysfunction, the behavior was labeled hyperactive child syndrome in the 1940s and then, more formally, hyperkinetic reaction of childhood (DSM-II) in 1968.

The first mention of ADD as a disorder was in the third edition of the *Diagnostic and Statistical Manual of Mental Disorders* (DSM-III) in 1980. The definition of ADHD encompassed only the hyperactive symptoms. The subtypes hyperactive and combined were diagnosable as neuropathic disorders, but subtype inattentive was not. The differences are outlined below, as referenced by the DSM:

How the Diagnostic Criteria for Adult ADHD Has Evolved

DSM-III (1980)
Name changed from hyperkinetic syndrome (1968) to attention deficit disorder;
Inattentiveness central to diagnosis;
More emphasis placed on impulsiveness;
Can be diagnosed without hyperactivity.

DSM-III-R (1987)
For the first time, included formal classification into adulthood;
For adults, required symptom onset in childhood;

More emphasis on overactivity than DSM-III;
Name changed to attention deficit hyperactivity disorder.

DSM-IV (1994)

Impulsive and hyperactive symptoms in same list but
identified separately;
Distinction between inattention and other symptom clusters.

seem distracted or fidgety. But if the doctor were to ask about work and home and how his employer or wife perceives things— symptoms and the settings in which they occur—the answers would be revealing.

Co-conditions

As we have discussed in chapter 3, it is estimated that 50 to 75 percent of all adults with ADHD have at least one coexisting condition.

The most common mental health disorders that adults with ADHD suffer from include major depression, bipolar disorder, dysthymia, and substance abuse. Substance abuse and dysthymia are among the most frequently observed. Dysthymia is a chronic depressed mood disturbance that fits certain clinical criteria for depression, but not all the criteria to be classified as a major depressive disorder. It is usually characterized by depressed mood, lethargy, pessimism, isolation, and detachment. Other comorbid conditions include anxiety disorders, personality disorders, antisocial behavior, and learning disabilities (dyslexia and auditory processing deficits), which coexist more than 20 percent of the time.

Again, the important point is that doctors need to recognize ADHD and the co-occurring conditions and attempt to decipher which symptoms are from ADHD and which are from the coexisting condition. Generally, the age of onset and longitudinal nature of symptoms is helpful. ADHD symptoms tend to be more or less present throughout an individual's life and have their roots in early childhood. Comorbid symptoms of a mood or substance abuse disorder tend to be more episodic and often have onset later than early childhood.

As you can see, making a diagnosis is tougher than it seems. In the rest of this chapter, I'll walk you through the methods and tools qualified doctors use to make the call.

How a Doctor Makes the Diagnosis

Extensive media coverage has increased public awareness of ADHD in children and also prompted many adults to seek a similar diagnosis, especially the parents of children diagnosed with ADHD. When adults learn about the hallmark symptoms of childhood ADHD, many recognize that they too were plagued by the same behaviors as children. For many, the knowledge that the disorder is hereditary and persists into adulthood prompts them into self-referral for a positive diagnosis and treatment. Unfortunately, less than 40 percent of those who are actually afflicted with ADHD are diagnosed, leaving many people undiagnosed.

As mentioned above, the four criteria for a positive diagnosis are: (1) the severity and frequency of symptoms; (2) the establishment of childhood onset of symptoms; (3) the chronicity and pervasiveness of symptoms; and (4) the impact of symptoms on major life activities.

Although these criteria may seem straightforward, the nature of the disorder and how it manifests over a lifetime can make it difficult to positively nail down from case to case. This is compounded by the fact that the process by which diagnosis is made is not objective (black-and-white), but subjective because it relies on the testimony of patients and their families.

The diagnosis process includes clinical interviews, rating scales, informant ratings of the patient, and objective supporting evidence. Analysis of the information, or data, gathered from these interviews and questionnaires are based on the perception and judgment of the patients, the other interviewees, and the attending physician, as opposed to more empirical data such as blood tests, urine analyses, and bone density scans. Perception and memory abilities can considerably alter how a person remembers their past or perceives the world around them. Symptoms can easily be either over- or underestimated. The key to diagnosing a disorder such as ADHD from other people's collective memories and perceptions is for the physician to identify and chronicle patterns of behavior exhibited by the patient that are consistent with ADHD.

Verifying Childhood Onset and Other Family Occurrences

ADHD is defined by onset during early childhood. Consequently, a positive diagnosis of adult ADHD can be established only if the adult has been suffering from some form of these symptoms since childhood. This criterion requires the clinician to obtain a detailed oral history from the patient to chronicle their symptoms since childhood.

Because there is a strong genetic component to the disorder—a 50 percent chance of its appearance in close relatives—the clinician must inquire about family history as corroborating evidence for a positive diagnosis.

Rating Scales

ADHD rating scales are increasingly considered to be the most accurate method of diagnosing the disorder—although no one scale is 100 percent accurate. Rating scales have been developed to help quantify and clarify the severity and frequency of the symptoms of ADHD sufferers. They are useful because they are standardized and they provide structure for probing patients for symptom-related information. For clinicians with limited experience in diagnosing ADHD, these standardized rating scales provide reliable tests for an accurate accounting of symptoms and assistance in making the diagnosis of ADHD. These scales also provide the most objective means of "rating" symptoms and, because they are standardized, measuring the response of patients to treatment. Most important, they have been demonstrated to be reliable in establishing the severity of the symptoms presented by an adult with ADHD. Since the expression of these symptoms changes over time, the challenging part is recognizing how they are expressed in adults. There are published guidelines to help physicians recognize ADHD symptomology.[3]

With respect to continuing research on ADHD, the results of these standardized rating scales provide large amounts of valuable data in a relatively short time. And the short, concise, and reliable questionnaires save time for both patients and clinicians in arriving at a correct diagnosis.

The rating scales available to you and your physician can be broken down into several categories: (1) screening tests to identify individuals at risk for ADHD; (2) symptom assessment scales, which can be patient- or doctor-admininstered; and (3) formal structured diagnostic scales. It is beyond the scope of this book to review these scales in detail, but we provide an overview and list resources where these scales are available to clinicians and patients.

Screening Tests

The Adult ADHD Self-Report Scale (ASRS v1.1) is a patient-administered test that queries the patient about the symptoms of adult ADHD. It comes in two forms: a six-item screening test and a full, eighteen-item symptom checklist (which includes the other twelve symptom domains in adult ADHD). These two scales (screener and symptom checklist) were established by a work group of experts on adult ADHD and are copyrighted by the World Health Organization (WHO). I was privileged to be part of the steering committee that guided the development of the ASRS v1.1. This committee was comprised of leading doctors from institutions including Harvard Medical School, Massachusetts General Hospital, New York University, Duke University, and Columbia University.

The eighteen symptoms of DSM-IV, which have been adapted to highlight the adult presentation of ADHD, give a context basis to the symptoms (such as settings in which symptoms might occur) and ask the questions in a manner in which patients can report their symptoms themselves. The ASRS (in both forms) has undergone extensive validation in studies conducted with patients with and without ADHD.[4]

The first four questions relate to inattentive symptoms, the last two to hyperactive-impulsive symptoms. Patients are asked to complete the screener themselves. If they have at least four of the six symptoms significantly, they are at high risk for ADHD. When we looked at the results of positive screens in patients with and without ADHD, it turned out that patients had a 93 percent chance of actually having ADHD when formal diagnostic interviews were performed.

Unlike the other rating scales, the developers of this screener focused on assessing the frequency of symptoms instead of the severity. The severity of symptoms is far more subjective and biased than the frequency because it is based on perception and the personal interpretation of each individual. The developers also expanded the rating scale to five potential responses (Never, Rarely, Sometimes, Often, Very Often) instead of the usual three or four (see below). One difference from other scales in response strategy is the distinction of "Never" and "Rarely." The ASRS distinguishes between them because the developers recognized that "Never" and "Rarely" reflect differing symptom frequencies. Another change in the ASRS is that the wording was designed specifically for adults, and not for symptoms in childhood or adolescence as is commonly employed in other scales.

Please remember that the ASRS v1.1 Screener does not provide a formal diagnosis but identifies individuals who are highly likely to have adult ADHD. The diagnosis can only be made by sitting down with your doctor and reviewing your symptoms and impairments as an adult and in childhood and also exploring for the presence of other mental health disorders.

After using the ASRS v1.1 Screener, clinicians will typically administer the remaining twelve questions in the ASRS symptom checklist, which gives a full survey of the adult manifestations of the eighteen items in DSM-IV. The clinician can then use this as a

The ASRS-v1.1 Screener

I. INATTENTION

	NEVER	RARELY	SOMETIMES	OFTEN	VERY OFTEN
How often do you have trouble wrapping up the fine details of a project, once the challenging parts have been done?	0	1	2*	3*	4*
How often do you have difficulty getting things in order when you have to do a task that requires organization?	0	1	2*	3*	4*
How often do you have problems remembering appointments or obligations?	0	1	2*	3*	4*
When you have a task that requires a lot of thought, how often do you avoid or delay getting started?	0	1	2	3*	4*

II. HYPERACTIVITY-IMPULSIVITY

	NEVER	RARELY	SOMETIMES	OFTEN	VERY OFTEN
How often do you fidget or squirm with your hands or your feet when you have to sit down for a long time?	0	1	2	3*	4*
How often do you feel overly active and compelled to do things, like you were driven by a motor?	0	1	2	3*	4*

ASRS-v1.1 Screener copyright © 2003 World Health Organization (WHO). Reprinted with permission of WHO. All rights reserved.

Asterisk (*) indicates significant symptoms.

road map to probe the extent of these symptoms and the resulting impairments.

Following is the eighteen-item ASRS Symptom Checklist:

Adult Self-Report Scale (ASRS-v1.1) Symptom Checklist

Patient Name   **Today's Date**

Please answer the questions below, rating yourself on each of the criteria shown using the scale on the right side of the page. As you answer each question, place an X in the box that best describes how you have felt and conducted yourself over the past 6 months. Please give this completed checklist to your healthcare professional to discuss during today's appointment.

	NEVER	RARELY	SOMETIMES	OFTEN	VERY OFTEN

PART A

1. How often do you have trouble wrapping up the final details of a project, once the challenging parts have been done? □ □ □ □ □

2. How often do you have difficulty getting things in order when you have to do a task that requires organization? □ □ □ □ □

3. When you have a task that requires a lot of thought, how often do you avoid or delay getting started? □ □ □ □ □

4. How often do you have problems remembering appointments or obligations? □ □ □ □ □

5. How often do you fidget or squirm with your hands or feet when you have to sit down for a long time? □ □ □ □ □

6. How often do you feel overly active and compelled to do things, like you were driven by a motor? □ □ □ □ □

PART B

7. How often do you make careless mistakes when you have to work on a boring or difficult project? □ □ □ □ □

8. How often do you have difficulty keeping your attention when you are doing boring or repetitive work? □ □ □ □ □

	NEVER	RARELY	SOMETIMES	OFTEN	VERY OFTEN
9. How often do you have difficulty concentrating on what people say to you, even when they are speaking to you directly?	☐	☐	▣	▣	▣
10. How often do you misplace or have difficulty finding things at home or at work?	☐	☐	☐	▣	▣
11. How often are you distracted by activity or noise around you?	☐	☐	▣	▣	▣
12. How often do you leave your seat in meetings or other situations in which you are expected to remain seated?	☐	☐	▣	▣	▣
13. How often do you feel restless or fidgety?	☐	☐	▣	▣	▣
14. How often do you have difficulty unwinding and relaxing when you have time to yourself?	☐	☐	▣	▣	▣
15. How often do you find yourself talking too much when you are in social situations?	☐	☐	☐	▣	▣
16. When you're in a conversation, how often do you find yourself finishing the sentences of the people you are talking to, before they can finish them themselves?	☐	☐	▣	▣	▣
17. How often do you have difficulty waiting your turn in situations when turn taking is required?	☐	☐	☐	▣	▣
18. How often do you interrupt others when they are busy?	☐	☐	▣	▣	▣

If you screen positive on the six-question screener, it's time to visit your doctor for a formal diagnosis. I would suggest taking the eighteen-question checklist with you.

The ASRS-v1.1 Screener and symptom checklist are available on the WHO, Harvard School of Public Health, and NYU School of

Medicine Adult ADHD Program Web sites (http://www.med.nyu
.edu/psych/psychiatrist/adhd.html).

Symptom Assessment Scales

There are a variety of scales that have been developed to assess current ADHD symptoms. They are catalogued in the chart below,
which reviews the major symptom assessment instruments:

Adult ADHD Instruments Symptom Assessment

Scale	Scale available from:
Brown ADD Scale	*The Psychological Corporation*
Conners Adult ADHD Rating Scale for DSM-IV	*Multi Health Systems, Inc.*
Wender-Reimherr Adult Attention Deficit Disorder Scale	*Fred W. Reimherr, M.D., Mood Disorders Clinic, Department of Psychiatry, University of Utah Health Science Center, Salt Lake City, Utah*
ADHD Rating Scale	*Guilford Press*
Barkley Current Symptoms Scale	*Barkley RA, Murphy KR. Attention-Deficit Hyperactivity Disorder: A Clinical Workbook. Second Edition.*
Adult Self-Report Scale v1.1	*www.med.nyu.edu/Psych /psychiatrist/adhd.html and the WHO Web site.*
Adult Investigator Symptom Report Scale (AISRS)	*Lenard Adler, M.D. Adult ADHD Program, New York University (NYU) School of Medicine adultADHD@med.nyu.edu*

Adler L, M.D., and Cohen J, B.A., "Diagnosis and evaluation of adults with attention-deficit/hyperactivity disorder," *Psychiatric Clinics of North America.* 2004(27):187–201.

We will not review the details of all of these scales but will discuss some of their similarities and differences.

Some of these scales are clinician-administered (AISRS, Wender-Reimherr Adult ADD Scale, and Barkley Current Symptoms Scale), some have patient- and clinician-administered versions (Conners Adult ADHD Rating Scale for DSM-IV), some can be administered by either the clinician or the patient (Brown ADD Scale and ADHD Rating Scale), and some are solely patient-administered (ASRS-v1.1 Symptom Checklist). As noted above, the ASRS-v1.1 provides a context basis for symptoms. Some of the scales are confined to eighteen core symptom domains in DSM-IV (ASRS-v1.1 Symptom Checklist, AISRS, and ADHD Rating Scale), while others examine some of the ancillary symptoms of ADHD, including deficits in executive function and mood regulation (Conners Adult ADHD Rating Scale, Brown ADD Scale, Wender-Reimherr Adult ADD Scale, and the Barkley Current Symptoms Scale).

The AISRS, developed by experts at Massachusetts General Hospital and NYU School of Medicine, contains a set of questions about adult ADHD, termed "prompts," which are available through the NYU School of Medicine. Many physicians find these prompts helpful in engaging their patients in a dialogue about their illness. The prompts are intended to allow your doctor to more fully probe the extent and impact of adult ADHD symptoms.

The prompts look something like the box on the next page (which has partial lists of prompts for several adult ADHD symptom domains).

Another use of symptom assessment scales, beyond an initial catalogue of adult ADHD symptoms, is that they can be used by your doctor to objectify your symptom changes during the course of treatment. This can help measure your improvement.

Some Questions Your Doctor Might Ask

Careless mistakes

- Do you make a lot of mistakes in school or at work?
- Is this because you're careless?
- Do you have trouble with detailed work?

Difficulty sustaining attention

- Do you have trouble paying attention, such as watching movies, reading, or at lectures?
- Or during fun activities such as sports or board games?
- Is it hard for you to keep your mind on school or work?

On the go/acts like driven by motor

- Is it hard for you to slow down?
- Do you feel like you (often) have a lot of energy and that you always have to be moving, are always "on the go"?

© Massachusetts General Hospital and New York University School of Medicine

Diagnostic Scales

A variety of diagnostic scales have been developed to help your doctor go beyond identifying symptoms and guide him/her through the process of making a full DSM-IV diagnosis of ADHD. These scales have all been validated in diagnostic studies in patients with and without ADHD and are shown in the table below.

The Kiddie-SADS Diagnostic Interview ADHD Module uses childhood-specific prompts to establish the presence and severity of childhood symptoms of ADHD. The ACDS v1.2 uses these childhood prompts to document the childhood onset of the disorder

Adult ADHD Diagnostic Scales

Scale	Scale available from:
Conners Adult ADHD Diagnostic Interview for DSM-IV	*Multi Health Systems, Inc.*
Barkley Current Symptoms Scale with supplemental Barkley scales	*Barkley RA, Murphy KR. Attention-Deficit Hyperactivity Disorder: A Clinical Workbook. Second Edition.*
Brown ADD Scale Diagnostic Form	*The Psychological Corporation*
Kiddie-SADS Diagnostic Interview ADHD Module	*www.wpic.pitt.edu/ksads*
Adult ADHD Clinician Diagnostic Scale (ADCS) vl.2	*Lenard Adler, M.D., Adult ADHD Program, New York University (NYU) School of Medicine adultADHD@med.nyu.edu*

and the adult ADHD prompts, the ones used in the AISRS discussed above, to establish the severity and impact of adult ADHD symptoms. The Conners Adult ADHD Diagnostic Interview for DSM-IV (CAADID) uses a similar cataloguing of adult and childhood symptoms with its own set of cues. Most of the recent clinical trials in adult ADHD have used the CAADID or ACDS v1.2 to establish the diagnosis of adult ADHD.

OBJECTIVE EVIDENCE AND SYMPTOMS

As useful and reliable as these symptom assessment scales can be, it is recommended that they not be used as the sole means of diagnosis. These self-reports rely heavily on the patient's recall of childhood symptoms and cannot conclusively establish that the symptoms have persisted since childhood, the principal criterion of ADHD. Hence, these rating scales should be used only as tools and not as definitive sources of evidence for a positive diagnosis of ADHD.

Clearly, the opportunity for an accurate diagnosis of ADHD increases when the physician seeks corroborating evidence of the presence and frequency of the symptoms through interviews with family, employers, friends, and previous doctors. The information gleaned from these oral histories them helps establish a pattern of behavior and the presence of life-activity impairment, and serves to eliminate other causes of the symptoms, such as laziness or poor vocational habits, a transient situation, or even environmental circumstances.

Neuropsychological Testing

Neuropsychological testing, which is used in about 20 percent of adults presenting for ADHD evaluations, has been shown to be helpful in a variety of cases where self-reporting is deemed unreliable or potentially inaccurate. In neuropsychological testing a patient's cognitive abilities, memory, and motor skills are assessed through a variety of tests. Practitioners generally use neuropsychological testing in the following situations: where a diagnosis from childhood is not definitive or obtainable; where there is an elevated uncertainty of a diagnosis of ADHD versus a comorbid condition; and where there is a diagnostic concern of adult ADHD as opposed to a learning disability. Neuropsychological testing in adults is different from that in children, where it is commonly employed to document the extent of ADHD symptoms and functional impairment for educational reasons. The neuropsychological tests used in ADHD are specific tests administered by a psychologist that examine attention (verbal and written/sustained and variable), recall, memory, reaction time, processing speed, impulse control, executive functions (including working memory [keeping things in mind] and awareness of an individual's relationship to their environment), and may also include intelligence and achievement assessments. Neuropsychological tests are somewhat limited in their clinical utility as only one in two to one in three of the patients with adult ADHD actually have significant deficits documented by this testing. This does not mean that individuals without deficits on neuropsychological testing do not have ADHD, but rather that their deficits were not picked up by these batteries of tests. Nevertheless, neuropsychological testing should be used in the circumstances I described above as it clearly plays a role in the workup of adult ADHD in those situations.

It is important to remember that neuropsychological tests are like any other test in clinical medicine—they do not provide a diagnosis by themselves, but can provide highly useful information that the doctor can integrate into the clinical evaluation. Finally, if neuropsychological testing is being used for an adult with ADHD in order to document impairment to obtain accommodations for educational reasons (on graduate-level exams or in college or graduate school), I recommend that the clinician performing the testing review the specific requirements of that institution or testing authority, as they can vary quite a bit.

An Accurate Diagnosis Is Worth the Effort

As you can see, getting an accurate diagnosis for a disorder as complex and difficult to recognize as adult ADHD isn't always easy. But doing so is the first, essential step in getting the help you need to manage the condition. If you don't feel your doctor is handling your concerns with the close care and attention you deserve, seek out other medical help. The resource section at the back of this book can help point you in the right direction. Most of all, don't give up until you get the answers and help you need. I can assure you that your well-being will be well worth the effort.

CHAPTER SIX

Medications That Can Help

Getting a Diagnosis Is the First Step

As I've said throughout this book, a correct diagnosis from a qualified professional is the critical first step in getting help. As discussed in the previous chapter, the recognition of ADHD as a disorder in adults is a relatively new discovery in the medical field and is gaining wide acceptance—unlike ADHD in kids, which has been recognized and treated for years by pediatricians and psychiatrists alike. Because information about the symptoms of the adult disorder has only recently been made widely available to primary care physicians, many people remain undiagnosed and untreated. Still others are diagnosed with other disorders such as depression, anxiety, and anger management disorder, which may or may not be co-occurring with ADHD, or may be separate conditions altogether.

Since ADHD has become more widely known and publicized, the majority of adults who seek medical help for symptoms of ADHD are self-referred. Many have started to realize that the symptoms they have had all their lives might have roots in childhood and seek treatment on their own accord. As we've discussed, the most common symptoms that give people pause include poor concentration, disorganization, poor time-management skills, a tendency to leave projects incomplete, inattentiveness, poor academic and work performance, impulsiveness, and changeable moods.

An Increasingly Common Course of Treatment

Today, more adults than ever are being treated for ADHD—an increase from 0.5 percent of all adults to 1 percent. This is not surprising given the recent attention on the disorder in adults. Even with this doubling of adults seeking help and treatment, more than three-quarters of those with the disorder are untreated.[1]

It also appears that women are now being treated for ADHD in greater numbers. This is not surprising. Many of the symptoms in girls are initially overlooked because they don't manifest as broadly as in boys. So, unfortunately, many women have suffered quietly, or did not manifest the gross symptoms until later in life.

Getting a Baseline

Without patients reaching out to seek treatment for ADHD-like symptoms, successful diagnosis and treatment are very difficult. By the time ADHD children become adults, they may have developed effective coping skills, learned to conceal some of the symptoms, and/or recovered from diagnostic symptoms, such as hyperactivity, which diminishes at a faster rate over time than inattentiveness. It is only recently that primary care physicians have begun to chronicle these symptoms by asking patients if they had them as children because childhood ADHD behaviors and symptoms can persist into adulthood, despite what many people think. The oral histories taken are referred to as "retrospective accounts."

Armed with these historical overviews, the primary care physician has the opportunity to identify signature patterns of ADHD symptoms throughout the patient's life, and catalogue the progression of the disorder. This information contributes greatly to our understanding of how ADHD develops, and what treatments work and don't work over a lifetime.

As described in chapter 2, ADHD is manifested differently in each individual, making it very difficult to diagnose correctly without a historical accounting. For example, although depression can occur with ADHD, it is not a given for all adults with ADHD. You need to make a distinction between depressed mood (a feeling state) and depressive illnesses—dysthymia (chronic depression) and episodic depression in the context of recurrent unipolar or bipolar depression. With a list of eighteen symptoms for ADHD, the number of possible symptom combinations that a person can exhibit is astonishing. Again, this is where the retrospective history plays a significant role, because if a pattern of behavior extending from childhood can be established, the patient is one step closer to an accurate diagnosis and treatment.

ADHD Medications: An Overview

As we will discuss later in this chapter, the choice of medication is essentially between a stimulant—methylphenidate (Ritalin and others) or amphetamine (Adderall and others)—or a non-stimulant, primarily atomoxetine (Strattera). For adult patients we generally look to achieve treatment throughout much of the day, which is quite different from the goals for an elementary school-age child with ADHD, where medication can be administered by a parent or school nurse at intervals during the school and after-school period.

Generally long-acting, sustained-release stimulants are recommended for adults, as they have very long days, and the shorter-acting versions would require multiple dose administrations (the short-acting versions have duration of effects of three to five hours). It is difficult for any individual, with or without ADHD, to take medications on such a tight schedule—or they simply may not remember—especially since stimulant effects can wear off between doses if not timed correctly. Individuals may experience "rebound" effects in which ADHD symptoms return during any gaps between doses—more on this later.

We will discuss the specific medication choices in detail later in this chapter, but there is little "hard" data to help you and your doctor decide between a stimulant or non-stimulant medication, as both work well and there are few if any head-to-head comparisons between these medication classes. The choice of medication class is therefore part of the "art" form of treatment and one that should be clearly partnered with your doctor. Some overall guidelines might be helpful in this regard and are detailed below.

For example, if a patient was treated successfully in childhood, I'll use a similar medication. The idea is that if an individual improved with something once, then try it again. This isn't a fail-safe method, but it's often a good starting place. If there's a family member with a response to a medication, it might suggest a treatment option. I'll often speak with spouses or significant others. This information helps to piece together the puzzle and helps me, or another physician, better understand the patient.

Tom is a thirty-nine-year-old advertising executive who came in for an evaluation for adult ADHD when he was in the midst of a work crisis. He had just received a negative review for speaking out of turn and telling inappropriate jokes during meetings. He has a lifelong history of procrastination and trouble completing tasks, going all the way back to kindergarten. When he was an undergraduate he was on academic probation and had to change colleges. He works in advertising sales and has had trouble keeping jobs—changing jobs six times in six years. He is married, without children. His wife is well aware of his procrastination, impulsive talking, and trouble planning, all of which cause difficulty at home.

Tom experienced a depressive episode several years ago, which was successfully treated. With the medication he felt that his ADHD symptoms improved, but he was no longer taking the medication.

His ASRS-v1.1 symptom checklist revealed significant difficulties with completing projects, prioritizing, remembering appointments and obligations, attending to conversations, misplacing items, distraction, unwinding/relaxing, talking out of turn, and interrupting others. Also revealed was his tendency to always be on the go, as if motor-driven.

After receiving the diagnosis of ADHD, combined subtype, Tom started a course of medication and coaching. He is currently taking a combination of sustained-release (OROS) methylphenidate (Concerta), 36 mg/day, and atomoxetine HCl (Strattera) 60 mg/day, with significant improvement of his attentional symptoms. He is working on increasing his productivity at work with his improved ability to plan. He is now regarded as a valuable member of the team and is no longer facing a work crisis.

Coexisting Conditions Can Make Effective Treatment a Challenge

As we've discussed throughout this book, another difficulty in treating ADHD accurately is the phenomenon of coexisting conditions. For example, depression. Depression can be caused by different factors, including significant life stressors and/or biochemical imbalances. Although the "depression" that people express may be symptomatically similar, it does not originate from the same source, nor is it necessarily treated with the identical therapy. The subtle but very real distinctions between the origins of symptoms are difficult to detect, especially for physicians who have not known their patients since childhood.

As discussed, some of the most common disorders that accompany ADHD are depressive disorders, including major depression and chronic depression (dysthymia); bipolar disorder; anxiety disorders, including generalized anxiety disorder, panic disorder, and obsessive-compulsive disorder; and substance abuse or dependence disorders—the latter being of great concern in treating patients. As we have reviewed in the prior chapters, because coexisting conditions are the rule, not the exception, when treating an adult with ADHD, physicians must be aware of these issues and treat each existing condition. If the comorbid condition is likely to have a more significant impact on the patient, it should be treated before the ADHD. For example, if a patient has a comorbid major depression, which can be life-threatening, it should be treated first because the ADHD, although highly impairing and impactful, is not acutely life-threatening.

Coexisting conditions definitely influence the choice of medications used to treat ADHD. For example, for a patient with an active substance abuse or dependence problem, I will try a non-stimulant medication first to avoid any abuse liability in treatment. In this situation, however, I strongly encourage the patient to get treatment for substance abuse. In fact, studies have shown that medication treatment for ADHD will fail unless the patient is actively enrolled and engaged in substance-abuse treatment.

It's a little like the chicken-and-egg conundrum: If you don't treat ADHD, you have an increased risk for substance abuse. We know that up to 50 percent of untreated ADHD adults have a history of drug or alcohol abuse problems or dependence, which is disturbing. But the upside is that early treatment of ADHD gives us the opportunity to slow or stop the onset of substance abuse, which will greatly improve the patient's overall health and well-being. In individuals with a history of substance abuse who are sober, treatment of ADHD can help prevent a relapse.

Treatment Strategies for ADHD

While diagnosing and treating adults with ADHD is a fairly new development in medicine, we have seen many positive results. So far, successful management of ADHD in adults is generally accomplished through the use of medication, possibly in combination with behavioral therapy or coaching. Choosing the treatment protocol for each patient is based on a myriad of variables: the subtype of ADHD the patient expresses (inattentive, hyperactive-impulsive, or combined), the symptoms the patient most wants to mitigate, optimizing the length of treatment throughout the day, whether or not the patient has other conditions that need to be considered (substance abuse, bipolar disorder, etc.), and the cultural perceptions about the medications available to ADHD sufferers.

Unlike in children, adults with ADHD have been struggling with their symptoms all their lives, and in most cases they have gone untreated. Although some of their symptoms may have dissipated by the time they seek help, others have become magnified, and many people have acquired psychological disorders or substance abuse problems in response to years of frustration and dysfunction. So the patient needs treatment not only for ADHD, but also for any other disorders they may have.

Interestingly, self-referred adults seem to be acutely aware of many of their symptoms and often have researched treatment options. The advances in information technology have helped patients become more sophisticated consumers, which is a great thing. When seeking medical attention, patients often come in prepared to discuss which symptoms they are most interested in having treated and generally the kind of medication they will and will not consider taking.

Further challenging the treatment strategy for adults are their occupations. Clearly construction workers or anyone who works with heavy or potentially dangerous equipment should not be prescribed a drug that could make them drowsy, or even one that could make them anxious.

Medication Works

Happily, physicians have found that the effects of medication on ADHD are pronounced. In fact, patients generally have a 70 percent chance of getting better from the first medication they take.

While there is no accepted treatment paradigm for adults, medication is a primary focus in treatment plans. Studies have found that medication yields results for most adults. Today, medication choices provide the equilibrium and support that many patients need to get back on their feet and move forward. Many patients ask me if taking medication is going to be a lifelong endeavor. For many, the answer is no. But taking medication for ADHD is a long-term prospect. Do you take it for the rest of your life? In most cases, no, but it may be for significantly longer than you might have originally imagined.

The most important factor for success is to find a doctor who can establish the diagnosis; then the patient must partner with that doctor to establish the optimal treatment paradigm, including type of medication, dosage, and follow-up plan. After about a year or so of treatment, you might be able to lower the dose and should continue to be carefully monitored. Over time, you and your doctor might find that the dose can be lowered again, or possibly even discontinued. However, most individuals who stop the medication begin to experience symptoms again and will need longer-term treatment—so it's essential to be carefully monitored.

Medications for Adult ADHD

For the most part, the medications used to treat adult ADHD affect mainly neurotransmissions of catecholamines. Catecholamines are a group of organic compounds produced in the body that function as hormones or neurotransmitters, or both. The catecholamines of interest are called dopamine and norepinephrine.

A variety of medical treatments are available and are used effectively, based on the patient's needs and medical history. The majority have few bothersome side effects, although all have been shown to have minor influences on pulse and blood pressure.

Physicians have been treating children with ADHD for more than sixty years. Benzedrine (an amphetamine) was used beginning in 1937 as a treatment for hyperkinetic children. This was used prior to other medications for mental health disorders, including antidepressants. A great deal of progress has been made in recent years from the short-acting stimulant medications widely used just a few years ago. Tricyclic antidepressants became the next popular treatment as an alternative to stimulants. The treatments were effective, and continue to be, but the side effects of tricyclic antidepressants caused great concern in children.

It wasn't until around 2000 when the landscape of alternative therapies for ADHD changed. New antidepressants, time-released stimulants, and non-stimulant drugs, such as atomoxetine, have come on the market. These newly available pharmacological therapies have provided doctors with more opportunities to tailor treatment regimes for their patients. This greatly improves the potential for success because some medications treat some patients better than others, and patients can make choices to fit their needs as well.

Although the dictum is that in general medication that works for children with ADHD also works for adults, ADHD treatments have been studied more extensively in children because the adult form of the illness has only recently come to light. Several medications have undergone the rigor of multi-center clinical registration trials to obtain FDA approval to date. These include Adderall XR and Focalin XR for the stimulants and atomoxetine (Strattera), a non-stimulant. The other medications we will discuss have been shown in scientific studies to have positive effects in adult ADHD but do not have FDA approval. Their use is "off-label"—meaning they are marketed medications for children or other conditions and have been shown to improve adult ADHD symptoms. Your physician can prescribe them to treat ADHD, but they are not approved by the FDA.

Let me detail overall guidelines for choosing stimulant or non-stimulant medication. Stimulants tend to have greater magnitude and earlier onset compared to non-stimulants. The stimulant effects can be seen within the first day of therapy (but are maximized over a period of weeks of dose adjustment), while it takes several weeks to observe maximal effects of non-stimulants after the dose is initiated or increased. Stimulants will have effects for a proscribed period of time throughout the day and then wane—in some way, each day is a new day with stimulants as patients awaken without significant levels of stimulants in their blood. Non-stimulants tend to have a longer titration period (as noted based on the time needed to maximize effects), but most experts believe they have potentially more regular effects throughout the course of the day. The non-stimulant atomoxetine has *not* been shown to have abuse liability or to worsen/induce tics (involuntary motor movements or vocal expressions). For patients with active substance abuse problems or tic disorders, treatment with atomoxetine should be considered the initial option.

Medications Used in Adult ADHD

Medication (generic)	Medication (brand)	Daily Dose[A] (mg)
Stimulants		**General Guidelines**
Methylphenidate	Ritalin	20–80
	Metadate CD	10–80
	Concerta	18–90
	Ritalin LA	10–80
d-Methylphenidate	Focalin	10–40
Extended-release d-methylphenidate	Focalin XR**	10–40
Dextroamphetamine	Dexedrine	10–60
	Dexedrine SR	10–60
Mixed amphetamine salts	Adderall	10–70
	Adderall XR**	10–70
Noradrenergic Agent		
Atomoxetine	Strattera	40–100
Antidepressants		
Tricyclics (TCA)	Norpramin,	100–300;
Desipramine;	Tofranil,	100–300
imipramine; nortriptyline	Pamelor	50–150
Bupropion	Wellbutrin SR	150–400
	Wellbutrin XL	150–450
Venlafaxine	Effexor	75–225
	Effexor XR	75–225

[A]Denotes typical daily doses. **FDA-approved for adults at up to 20mg/day (studies have shown efficacy at higher doses).
(Daily dose is final daily dose after careful titration.)

Daily Dosage Schedule	Common Adverse Side Effects
Three to four times	• Insomnia
	• Decreased appetite/weight loss
	• Headache
Once or twice	• Dysphoria
Once	• Rebound phenomena (short-acting preparations)
Once	• Mild increases in pulse/blood pressure
Once	
	• Tic induction or exacerbation
Two to three times	Note that these side effects are for all stimulants
Two to three times	
Once	
Once or twice	• Sleep disturbance
	• GI distress, nausea
	• Headache
	• Mild increase in pulse/blood pressure
Once or twice	• Dry mouth, constipation
	• Weight loss
	• Vital sign and ECG changes
Twice	• Irritability, insomnia
Once	• Risk of seizures (in doses > 6 in doses > 450 mg/day)
	• Contraindicated in bulimics
Twice	• Nausea
	• Sedation
	• GI distress

Stimulant medications rarely induce/exacerbate tics, and patients should be monitored for this side effect by their doctor. Recent data has shown that some patients with tic disorders can be safely treated with stimulants, but they probably should receive a trial of atomoxetine first and will need to be carefully monitored. Additionally, research has shown that dosing of stimulants and atomoxetine is somewhat weight-dependent, so it is not realistic to expect adults to respond to identical doses as children.

Treatment failure is commonly attributed to inadequate dosing. You need to take the right dose of a medication for a sufficient length of time to give it a fair chance to work.

Stimulants

This class of drugs acts on the areas of the brain that control attention, impulse, and self-regulating behavior. They stimulate the central nervous system by regulating the release and reuptake of norepinephrine/dopamine in the brain.

Stimulants have been known to be effective in mitigating ADHD symptoms for decades. At least 70 percent of children and adults respond positively to stimulants. Common side effects of these drugs include insomnia, decreased appetite/weight loss, headaches, and edginess. Blood pressure and pulse effects need to be monitored for both stimulants and atomoxetine. Stimulant medications are a mainstay of the pharmacotherapy for adults with ADHD and their use should be carefully balanced with the potential risks versus the possible dramatic life-changing positive effects. In August 2006 the FDA issued new warnings on stimulants used for ADHD. The black-box warning on amphetamines notes two issues: the potential for abuse and diversion, and the potential for sudden death and serious cardiovascular effects if the drug is misused. The warning on methylphenidate products highlights the need to use stimulant medications with caution in individuals with pre-existing cardiac conditions and that blood pressure and pulse should be followed during treatment. The decision to use stimulant medications should be partnered with your treating physician and your primary-care physician as appropriate.

Stimulants are generally considered "clean" in terms of drug interactions, meaning there are few issues or concerns with prescribing a stimulant medication for an individual who is taking other medications. However, persons with ADHD who also have active coexisting substance abuse problems generally should not be prescribed stimulant medications as they are potentially abusable.

METHYLPHENIDATES

Like their cousins the amphetamines, methylphenidates are norepinephrine and dopamine uptake inhibitors and increase the release of norepinephrine and dopamine in the brain.

The most widely known methylphenidate used to treat ADHD is Ritalin. Ritalin has been on the market for more than fifty years.

The sustained-release forms of methylphenidates include Concerta (methylphenidate), Ritalin LA (methylphenidate), and Focalin XR (extended-release d-methylphenidate). Concerta has a sustained duration of effect through controlled release of medication by an osmotic membrane. Focalin XR and Ritalin LA use beaded sustained-release mechanisms. Focalin XR is the newest addition to methylphenidates and is the active half of methylphenidate. That means that the inactive part of the Ritalin compound, which may contribute to unwanted side effects, is not present in Focalin.

The real difference between these methylphenidate drugs is

their delivery systems—that is, the rate of release of the drug into the bloodstream and its uptake in the brain. Ritalin is a multidose-a-day medication that comes in several dose availabilities. The regular-release Ritalin dosage is quick-acting and must be taken two to three times a day, thirty to forty-five minutes before a meal. The extended-release dosage lasts up to eight hours and can be taken twice a day. Focalin immediate-release is a two- to three-times-a-day medication; the doses are taken four to five hours apart, while Focalin XR has a duration of effect of ten to fourteen hours. Concerta is taken every nine or twelve hours (once a day). The effects of Ritalin LA last approximately eight hours, and Metadate CD seven to eight hours.

Ruby, a twenty-nine-year-old actress, waitress, and student, requested an evaluation of ongoing problems with inattention, restlessness, disorganization, planning, and task completion. She had voiced similar complaints to primary-care and psychiatric providers, and her decision to again seek a professional opinion was inspired by her sister's and her nephew's recent diagnoses with ADHD and their successful treatment. At seven, Ruby had herself been diagnosed with ADHD—and had also shown symptoms of a disruptive behavior disorder—but had not been treated per parental preference. As an adult, she had been diagnosed with depression alone and had received unsuccessful trials of the selective serotonin reuptake inhibitors fluoxetine and sertraline.

Ruby's retrospective reporting of symptoms showed significant impairment at school, at home, and among peers beginning at age six. As a child, Ruby was inattentive; her mother and her teachers often noted that she did not listen when spoken to. She showed impulsivity, as when she accidentally set the family house on fire trying to burn a tick off her pet dog. She ran about and climbed excessively, once fracturing her leg while leaping from furniture. Ruby's childhood fidgeting and hyperactivity made it difficult for her to sit still long enough to complete her homework.

As a young adult, she remained impulsive, once receiving a speeding ticket for driving over one hundred miles an hour in a borrowed sports car. In a typical progression, Ruby's childhood restlessness had evolved into an adult need to be always on the move, planning her daily activities to avoid situations that would require waiting, and taking active vacations. At the time of her initial visit, Ruby was forgetful and chronically late, which affected her work as an actress. She interrupted others and was distracted, which affected not only her job as a waitress but her interpersonal relationships as well. She suffered from feelings of inadequacy linked to her impairment.

Ruby's family history of ADHD helped support the diagnosis. She was started on a course of mixed dextroamphetamine and amphetamine (also known as mixed amphetamine salts), resulting in prompt, substantial improvement in her ADHD symptoms and the resolution of her depression. When Ruby reported that she was forgetting to take her medication, she was switched to 40 mg of extended-release formulation in the morning and 20 mg of immediate-release formulation in the afternoon, with good results.

Of interest is the fact that Ruby's depression resolved with psychostimulant treatment. It may be that her depression was an affective consequence of untreated, impairing ADHD symptoms. Alternatively, it's possible that the depression was a primary condition that was improved by amphetamine therapy. Either way, Ruby experienced significant improvement in all aspects of her life, and she continues to grow and thrive.

AMPHETAMINE COMPOUNDS

Amphetamines, one of two classes of synthesized stimulant drugs, have long been used to treat ADHD, as well as other disorders such as depression and narcolepsy, the condition of frequently and unintentionally falling asleep. Previously, they had also been used for weight loss management treatment and should not be used that way. The best known amphetamines today are Adderall (a preparation made of mixed amphetamine salts), Adderall XR, and Dexedrine. The significant difference between Adderall and Adderall XR is how long the effects last: Adderall must be taken twice daily, whereas the XR formulation lasts ten to twelve hours. Amphetamines not only block the uptake of dopamine and norepinephrine, they also signal the body to release more of it, thus stimulating the release of neurotransmitters in the brain.

Amphetamines have been around for more than a hundred years. They were first synthesized in Germany in 1887, but the medical community did not know how to effectively use them as a treatment. In the 1920s, they were resurrected from the files and investigated as a potential treatment for numerous illnesses, including epilepsy, schizophrenia, alcoholism, and migraines. During these investigations, it was discovered that amphetamines raise blood pressure, enlarge respiratory passages, and stimulate the central nervous system. By the early 1930s they were the active ingredient in over-the-counter inhalers.

Amphetamines were also found to be effective in treating children with ADHD in 1937. Although they are stimulants and seem contraindicated for medicating hyperactivity symptoms, they have the opposite effect on people with ADHD—they calm them down. By 1937, amphetamines were available in tablet form by prescription.

Medication	Duration of action
Methylphenidate	
Ritalin, Methylin	3 hours
Focalin	3–4 hours
Focalin XR	10–14 hours
Concerta	10–12 hours
Ritalin LA	8 hours
Metadate CD	7–8 hours
Amphetamine	
Dexedrine	3–4 hours
Dexedrine SR	5–6 hours
Adderall	4–6 hours
Adderall XR	10–12 hours

Amphetamines such as short-acting Adderall are taken two to three times a day (the exception being Adderall XR, which is taken only once daily). The duration of effect of Adderall XR is about ten to twelve hours. Common side effects include insomnia, decreased appetite/weight loss, headaches, edginess, and mild increase in blood pressure. Individuals with a preexisting heart condition should not take Adderall unless prescribed by a cardiologist.

Non-stimulants

NOREPINEPHRINE REUPTAKE INHIBITORS

Atomoxetine, or Strattera, is the first non-stimulant medication approved by the FDA to treat ADHD. Like stimulants, atomoxetine inhibits the uptake of norepinephrine so that they increase norepinephrine activity in the brain. So far it has proved very effective in alleviating ADHD symptoms in children and adults all day with only a single or twice-daily dose. A small body of literature may indicate that the effects in twice-daily dosing are somewhat greater than those of once daily, but the medication is FDA approved for either dosing strategy. While slightly less strong than stimulants, its advantages over stimulants—aside from the addiction risk factor—

include longer durations of action, a lower risk of rebound, and a lower risk of induction of tics or psychosis. Atomoxetine has also been used for treating ADHD with coexisting conditions, especially for tic disorder and substance abuse. In some cases, if the response is inadequate or side effects are problematic, switching from once-daily to twice-daily dosing is helpful.

Strattera use must be carefully monitored and dose adjustments made if used in patients taking the antidepressants fluoxetine (Prozac) or paroxetine (Paxil), as these medications influence the blood levels of Strattera. Also, it is not recommended for persons with acute angleglaucoma. Common side effects include sleep disturbance, gastrointestinal distress/nausea, headache, and mild increase in blood pressure. Rare side effects include reports of liver toxicity; FDA recommendations indicate that liver tests to screen for possible liver dysfunction in patients taking Strattera are not necessary, but that if flu-like symptoms and jaundice (yellowing of the skin) develop, the patient should immediately stop taking Strattera and contact their physician.

It is of note that studies have not found discontinuation syndromes or withdrawal symptoms when Strattera is stopped abruptly. Another rare side effect is the induction of suicidal thinking in children and adolescents. To quote from the warning label, "Strattera increased the risk of suicidal ideation in short-term studies in children or adolescents with ADHD. Anyone considering the use of Strattera in a child or adolescent must balance this risk with the clinical need. Patients who are started on therapy should be monitored closely for suicidality (suicidal thinking and behavior), clinical worsening, or unusual changes in behavior. Families and caregivers should be advised of the need for close observation and communication with the prescriber."

Betsy is a forty-seven-year-old elementary-school teacher who presented for an ADHD evaluation as she noted lifelong attentional issues, which she felt were similar to the issues that several children
with ADHD were experiencing in her classroom. Her ASRS-v1.1 symptom checklist revealed that she had significant inattentive issues with
easy boredom and drifting attention, not listening, organizational
problems, procrastination, and forgetting appointments. The only
hyperactive-impulsive symptoms present were difficulty waiting and
an impulse to interrupt others.

This pattern of having very prominent inattentive symptoms and a
few hyperactive-impulsive symptoms is not typical; even though Betsy
met symptom criteria for inattentive ADHD, she also had hyperactive-
impulsive symptoms that were not sufficient for her to meet criteria for
combined subtype.

These symptoms were present throughout her life history and
were often commented on by her parents and husband. She also was
having difficulty sitting with her two young daughters and helping
them with their homework. Betsy also felt that the difficulty with
task completion and planning had created significant difficulty at
work, often making her nervous about finishing things as they were
always left for the last minute.

We discussed that she did in fact have ADHD inattentive subtype
and started treatment trials sequentially with sustained-release
methylphenidate products (Concerta, Metadate CD), mixed amphetamine products (Adderall XR), and atomoxetine (Strattera). She
had a partial response of her symptoms to all of the stimulant trials,
but also developed some agitation. Betsy felt that Strattera in doses
up to 80 mg/day led to substantial improvement in her symptoms
without agitation. However, she felt sedated during the day, even

when she took her dose of Strattera in the evening. Attempts at treating her with combinations of stimulants and Strattera were unsuccessful as the sedation either persisted or she again felt "revved up." This sedation was improved with the alertness medication Provigil, which in combination with Strattera substantially improved her ADHD symptoms. These medication adjustments took place over a nine-month period, but Betsy feels that it was worth the investment of time to "get things right." Today she reports feeling more focused, relaxed, and productive than she's ever felt, and her family and friends note the improvements as well.

NICOTINE AND OTHER CHOLINERGIC AGENTS

Nicotine, a cholinergic stimulant, is known to have alleviating effects on adults with ADHD. A cholinergic stimulant works a bit differently from the norepinephrine uptake stimulants. These stimulants cause the ends of your nerve fibers to release acetylcholine, a neurotransmitter involved in the transmission of nerve impulses.

A short trial of patients using nicotine patches and other cholinergic medications demonstrated a significant reduction in ADHD symptoms and improved cognition; however, this form of treatment is not yet prevalent, nor is it FDA approved for adult ADHD. Cigarette smoking is dangerous to your health and the hope is that safe forms of administering these agents will be found in the future.

BUPROPION

Bupropion (Wellbutrin), an atypical antidepressant, has had good results on adult ADHD symptoms. Bupropion is considered helpful in treating ADHD with co-conditions such as mood instability, substance abuse, or biopolar disorder.[2] Historically the dose has been once or twice a day, but a relatively new formulation, Bupropion XL, is a once-daily preparation. Common side effects include insomnia and risk of seizures (in doses greater than 450 mg/day). Bupropion should not be given to bulimics or patients with seizure disorders.

Antidepressants

In addition to stimulants, antidepressants are used to treat patients with ADHD. Numerous classes of antidepressants have been used for children, including tricyclics, monoamine oxidase inhibitors, and various serotonin uptake inhibitors. Common tricyclic antidepressants include Norpramin or Pertofrane (desipramine), Tofranil (imipramine), Aventyl or Pamelor (nortiptyline), Adapin (doxepin), and Elavil (amitriptyline).

Tricyclic antidepressants are an older class of antidepressants (as compared to Prozac) whose chemical compound has three rings, hence the name. They are considered very effective, however, they can come with a host of unpleasant side effects (e.g., dry mouth, blurred vision, tremors, drowsiness). They interact badly with other medications, and when taken in excess, they can cause death. Tricyclic antidepressants work by preventing the brain's uptake of norepinephrine and serotonin, but they can have cardiac and hypertensive effects, which severely limit the practical use of these agents and are the reason they are rarely used. Serotonin is a neurotransmitter that stimulates smooth muscle, regulates cyclic body processes, and helps the transmission of impulses between nerve cells. The ensuing concentration of these two neurotransmitters improves communication between particular neurons, or nervous system cells. These agents generally need to be used in full antidepressant doses and SSRIs have not been shown to affect core ADHD symptoms, but might have an effect on comorbid depression or anxiety.

General doses are one to two times per day. Common side effects include dry mouth, constipation, vital sign and electrocardiographic changes, delaying the conduction of electrical impulses through the heart, and hypotensive effects. These significant side effects limit the usefulness of these medications.

Antihypertensive agents

Antihypertensive medications are prescribed to adults with ADHD to help reduce aggressiveness, temper outbursts, and marked hyperactivity. They are used primarily for impulse regulation. These medications lower noradrenergic tone like alpha agonists (clonidine—catapress or guanfacine—tenex) or beta-blockers (like propranolol-Inderal). There is limited evidence of their efficacy as a primary treatment for adult ADHD.

Antinarcoleptic/alertness medications

Alertness-enhancing medications such as Provigil, generally used to treat narcolepsy, are among the newest approaches to treating adult ADHD symptoms. Clinical trials have not fully established their efficacy in adult ADHD, although data has shown efficacy in children and may indicate a promising efficacy rate in mitigating symptoms of ADHD.

Combination Therapy

Combination therapy has been very successful with adults and children, including combining medications, and this is what I find most successful in treating my patients. Different medications and approaches can often correct different symptoms. By employing this broad approach to treatment, a patient's expectation for relief is greatly improved.

Simply put, adults have more complex lives than children, with more cognitively demanding tasks and longer days. Although stimulant and non-stimulant medications have been shown to be effective in treating adults, the unique, whole-life needs of the adult population require longer-acting medications. Longer-acting preparations of stimulant medications, such as methylphenidates and mixed short-acting stimulants, have made great strides toward meeting these needs. The addition of a short-acting stimulant acts to amplify the effects in the morning of the stimulant, and extend their therapeutic action later in the day.

Often, when a patient comes to me and doesn't have any mitigating factors to consider, I recommend stimulants or Strattera first, especially if the patient has profound symptoms. Stimulants provide robust symptom control and patients can see results in as early as one week.

Bob is a twenty-eight-year-old attorney who carries a heavy caseload. He came in for an ADHD evaluation after reading a newspaper article on the condition. He described ongoing issues with task completion, inattention, needing to reread material, drifting off in conversations, restlessness, finding time for himself, finishing people's sentences, and organization. The symptoms dated back to elementary school, where he felt he had skated by. He was diagnosed with ADHD in high school and received a brief trial of methylphenidate in high school and then intermittently in college.

Bob felt that he was impaired by these issues, in particular by losing focus in conversations at work and socially. His recent reviews at work were fairly positive, but noted his tendency to make careless mistakes. He felt the organizational issues were affecting him at home and that the attentional issues impaired his driving. He smoked a pack of cigarettes a day (and had done so for the last several years). His smoking had increased with increased demands at work. Bob had attempted to stop smoking on numerous occasions, but without success.

After reviewing with him his diagnosis of combined subtype ADHD and his treatment options, we agreed on a treatment trial of the long-acting OROS methylphenidate (Concerta). As his dose was gradually increased he noticed improvement in his attention, distractibility, and restlessness, and he no longer felt the urge to smoke. He was able to gradually decrease his smoking to the point where he stopped altogether on a Concerta dose of 72 mg in the morning.

Bob felt that to a large degree he had been self-medicating his ADHD with the nicotine. He did notice, however, that the medication wore off about ten hours after the morning dose. Since he worked long hours, this meant the attentional issues returned in the early evening. This issue was successfully tackled by adding a dose of the short-acting d-methylphenidate (Focalin) in the early evening, which provided symptom relief for an additional five hours.

An important take-home point from Bob's experience is that if you had looked at Bob's symptoms in the early evening, without being aware that the general duration of Concerta is nine to twelve hours, you might conclude that the medication was ineffective. But by supplementing the long-acting methylphenidate preparation with the short-acting d-methylphenidate (Focalin), Bob was able to get relief from his symptoms throughout the day.

When I prescribe a stimulant for an adult patient, I generally choose a long-acting agent first. Adults have long days and it's unrealistic to expect them to take a medication four to five times a day—something people with time-management issues simply can't do. I want to give my patients every opportunity for success, and this includes interfering as little as possible in their daily lives. If the duration of long-acting stimulants is insufficient, I will add a small dose of short-acting stimulant, as in Bob's case. (These medications are in the same "class" and are chemically similar in action, but differ in delivery system and duration of action.)

Another treatment strategy that some doctors employ is combining Strattera with long-acting stimulants, although there is only one case series reported to date documenting the efficacy of this approach. An advantage of this combination might be the potential benefits of increased efficacy and sustained effects. Although one small study in children did not find additive blood pressure effects from this combination, blood pressure should be carefully monitored with this combination therapy.

When non-stimulant medication is appropriate, I generally start with an 18- to 25-mg dose of Strattera and adjust from that point. It takes a bit longer to see results from a non-stimulant, and I ask patients to be patient: If you increase the dosage too aggressively, the patient will experience side effects. The upside of this medication is that it generally lasts throughout the day. So if I'm worried about a patient not taking medication regularly or forgetting the second dose, I may lean toward prescribing Strattera. There is also some data showing that individuals who have incomplete responses or trouble tolerating Strattera once daily may have improved effects and tolerability if the total Strattera dose is split into twice-daily dosing.

Charting Your Progress—Together

Symptom assessment scales (including the ASRS-v1.1 Symptom Checklist, ADHD RS, AISRS, and the Conners Adult ADHD Scale) are often used to monitor treatment response and to ensure that the patient sees at least a 30 percent reduction in overall symptoms. The scales also help to track the symptoms throughout the day, and how they affect work and home life. A careful review of these scales allows physicians to better modify treatments for the best results.

Of course, treatment isn't simply about symptom management. It is the first step toward whole-life improvement, which is why it is important for the doctor and patient to develop a relationship that will endure over the course of treatment. Treatment is not easy, however. Medication must be adjusted on a regular basis, both when the patient experiences side effects and when a new dose doesn't work. The chance of success is greatest if the patient has realistic expectations and is willing to give the medications a chance to work. The good news is that they often *do* yield results and offer patients a great deal of relief.

CHAPTER SEVEN

Complementary Treatments

Thanks to exciting advancements in medicine and great strides in understanding mental health disorders, people who suffer with ADHD today are far more fortunate than those who suffered with it twenty, ten, or even five years ago. Nonetheless, the fact remains that there is no "cure" for ADHD. Every day, science brings us closer to a time when a tried-and-true ADHD panacea will become available—but until then, treating the disorder remains an imperfect science. The good news is that there's a whole world of treatments in addition to medicinal ones that lies at your disposal. You may have heard of ADHD patients using cognitive behavioral therapy, coaching, or other forms of therapy. The key to finding the combination that will suit your individual needs is knowing which *safe* treatments have worked for others. This chapter outlines a few that have delivered positive results.

Complements, Not Replacements

Before we delve into the world of treatments known collectively as complementary and alternative medicine (CAM), it is important to understand why these treatments should be used to complement (and *not* to replace) the medication prescribed by your physician. Most medicines currently being prescribed in doctors' offices are backed by more than two decades of research. Abandoning the treatment recommended by your health care professional in favor of an alternative treatment can delay the benefits you would receive from medicine and, worse, unnecessarily prolong your suffering. As it stands, there is little to no hard scientific proof that nontraditional treatments can effectively treat ADHD on their own.

That being said, you may be wondering what makes complementary and alternative medicine such a popular option among ADHD sufferers.

Many people choose to complement their ADHD treatment with alternative medicine for personal reasons, and there are many. Medication should play a primary role in most treatment plans. As stated before, there is still much room for advancement in the science of treating ADHD with drugs. Some studies of stimulant medications have shown that between 20 and 30 percent of adults are nonresponders: They either experienced a very low reduction in symptoms after taking prescribed medicines or their bodies were unable to tolerate the drugs. Therefore, some people use CAM to enhance the effect of the medication or to condition their bodies to be more receptive to drug treatment. Some ADHD sufferers try CAM based on the recommendation of friends, relatives, or their health care providers. Though there is limited research that solidly supports the effectiveness of these treatments, most forms of popularly recommended complementary medicine have no negative side effects, so there is little harm in keeping an open mind. Some people simply have had good experiences with certain forms of

CAM, so they don't question why they work. They simply let the results speak for themselves.

In the absence of formal research, the effectiveness of combination treatments continues to be supported with anecdotal evidence, clinical experience, common sense, and accounts from patients themselves who have enjoyed the benefits.

When Does Complementary Medicine Help Most?

Complementary and alternative medicine has been described in various studies as the "art" behind dealing with ADHD, as opposed to the "science" (medicinal treatment). Many individuals are able to make meaningful life changes with medication alone; others find complementary treatments such as cognitive behavioral therapy and/or coaching facilitate the desired changes. Consider this analogy: You need to do research on the Internet but you've never used a computer. The medication is the computer. The ancillary therapy is the friend who shows you how to click on the mouse and save your work.

Medication is most effective in relieving the core symptoms of ADHD, but does not provide concrete strategies for meeting organizational goals or comfortably navigating a normal day. Many individuals are able to translate symptom improvements into real life changes. Once the symptoms are managed, some individuals need additional help to make real life changes.

Taking all this into consideration, it becomes clear that psychosocial therapies (cognitive behavioral therapy and coaching) are most effective for people who have stabilized as much as they can with medication. Complementary and alternative treatments can now be used to address the remaining problems—the stubborn symptoms unaffected by drugs, and poor symptom management skills. In short, complementary and alternative treatments are most effective when taken as a next-step treatment approach after a traditional, doctor-prescribed treatment is under way.

With that said, let's explore the various types of complementary and alternative treatments for ADHD. I have divided them into three categories: psychosocial treatments, alternative treatments, and mind/body treatments.

Psychosocial Treatments

The primary goals of psychosocial treatments are to help ADHD sufferers gain a better understanding of their disorder and how it specifically affects them, and subsequently to help them regain control over their lives using this knowledge. Psychosocial treatments focus on teaching ADHD sufferers how to solve the problems they encounter from day to day, how to set and reach goals, and how to deal with the feelings of depression or anxiety that often come with the disorder. A few of the most popular and effective types of psychosocial treatments are listed here.

Individual Supportive Psychotherapy

Many sufferers of ADHD constantly feel lost or misunderstood. They have questions about themselves, but they don't know where to seek answers. This is where individual supportive psychotherapy can prove very helpful. Individual psychotherapy helps ADHD sufferers gain insight into their disorder and can give them an understanding of how much of the hardship they face in their daily lives is due to ADHD and not to inherent flaws in their personalities.

Therapists are specially trained to help patients deal with emotions and overcome self-defeating beliefs. In many cases, tifying and understanding the source of problems gives patients great hope for identifiable solutions. After therapists help patients remove the barriers to their mental or emotional healing, they can seek out the solutions to their problems most effectively and thereby discover their own inner strength.

Typically with this kind of treatment, a person with ADHD sits down with a psychological health professional who helps him to understand how the disorder affects him every day. Many patients are surprised to discover how many daily activities ADHD impedes, and how many of the things they have always considered their personal "failures" can actually be traced back to their disorder. In the process of speaking regularly with a therapist, ADHD sufferers can build their self-esteem and take comfort in knowing that there is a place where it is perfectly fine and even desirable to discuss their worries and anxieties. The therapist is a reliable ally for the patient, as well as a knowledgeable guide.

Once the therapist has helped the patient to clarify questions, he or she can help the patient deal with any problems or crises that require immediate attention. The patient may be on the brink of losing their job or ending a relationship. In trying times such as these—when *anyone* would feel helpless or frustrated beyond rationality—a therapist can lend an ear when others may not listen or understand and help put things into perspective. Guided discussions that explore the reasons for the crisis lead to discussions of possible solutions. If no urgent problems exist, any ongoing problems that an ADHD patient may have will benefit from the same process of identification and discussion. In any case, a therapist can provide valuable problem-solving and coping strategies that patients might never have thought of implementing on their own.

Therapy is challenging for both the patient and the specialist, and positive results do not always appear as quickly as either would like. However, oftentimes patients can learn a lot about themselves and ADHD through individual psychotherapy. Also not to be over-looked is the comfort patients can receive from the full attention of a professional who is willing to listen and eager to help.

Cognitive Behavioral Therapy

Cognitive behavioral therapy (CBT), as the name implies, is a com-bination of two effective forms of therapy—cognitive therapy and behavioral therapy. Cognitive therapy focuses on showing a pa-tient how certain thinking patterns can be the cause of undesirable symptoms associated with their ADHD. Behavioral therapy shows a patient how to weaken the impulse to behave in certain habitual and destructive ways when stressful situations arise (for example, becoming extremely and visibly irritable or withdrawing from the world). Patients who undergo CBT can change their thinking pat-terns to minimize noticeable ADHD symptoms and can also con-dition themselves not merely to react to situations, but to think them through and behave in the way that is most appropriate. CBT essentially helps people with ADHD take control of their thoughts so they behave rationally and with a clear mind and specific ob-jectives or goals.

Unlike supportive psychotherapy, which focuses on instilling patients with personal insight and helping them through a long, in-trospective process of self-discovery, CBT works on arming ADHD patients with strategies that will make immediate differences in their lives. CBT also focuses on replacing negative mind-sets with positive and realistic thinking. Unlike an individual psychotherapist, the therapist who employs CBT is not especially concerned with guiding patients through self-discovery so they can find answers to their problems. Rather, cognitive behavioral therapists take a more active role in a patient's recovery. He or she will "diagnose" a patient's specific problems, formulate the proper solutions, and create a schedule or plan for the patient to implement those solutions. The benefit of this strategy is that both patient and specialist can see the results of the plan with their own eyes in a short period of time.

As in individual supportive psychotherapy, in CBT there is a certain level of patient education involved. This is necessary if patients are to understand the role their negative thought patterns have in hindering their ability to make changes. Mental health professionals who use CBT often explain to ADHD patients that not every one of their failures or setbacks is a result of their being impaired by the disorder. They show patients that *everyone* experiences daily hardships, and encountering snags on a daily basis is normal. There are proper ways to deal with every situation, and these hold true whether the person dealing with them is afflicted with ADHD or not. Once this understanding is reached, ADHD patients are often less likely to be convinced that the hardships they encounter have no solution. Not every barrier or obstacle needs to be a painful reminder of how they are different from everyone else. This new mode of thinking reduces an ADHD sufferer's tendency to regard difficult situations as being hopeless, and prompts them to actively seek solutions.

With CBT, patients learn that the solutions to many of their daily problems can come in the form of simple organizational and planning skills. These skills can significantly reduce the number and severity of daily hardships they encounter. For example, if an ADHD sufferer can devise a way to avoid losing her keys in the morning, she can avoid arriving late to work. Preventing this bad start to the workday will eradicate the frustration that would usually hinder productivity in the office. Contentment with work performance reduces the chance that a person will go home irritated or angry, and this in turn helps to minimize the number of unnecessary fights with family members that can occur as a result. Ultimately, all this can greatly reduce strains on relationships at the end of the day. As illustrated in this scenario, learning organizational skills can go a long way in improving an ADHD sufferer's feeling of well-being.

Cognitive behavioral therapists recognize the importance of good planning and organizational skills, and work to instill these skills in patients. They may show their patients how to rely on a personal planner to get through the day without missing appointments, meals, or tasks. Electronic planners or personal data assistants (PDAs) can prove extremely useful because they employ alarms or electronic alerts to remind the user of upcoming tasks or appointments. Additionally, therapists will show ADHD sufferers how to designate certain places in the house for keys, mail, and so on, so that fewer things are lost or misplaced. They teach patients how to break down large tasks into smaller, more manageable ones.

Because attention span is often a concern, cognitive behavioral therapists often methodically help patients to identify the length of their individual attention span. Once this is established, the professional can help the patient develop the habit of breaking tasks into chunks that take this amount of time. The key to effective behavioral therapy as part of CBT is to neutralize ADHD symptoms so they have minimal impact. Therapists show patients that as complicated and difficult as this may sound, there are very simple techniques to accomplish this. All that is required is clear structure and focus.

In accordance with cognitive therapy, therapists also teach patients techniques to stay calm and avoid panic when things go wrong, even when this happens in spite of their best efforts to remain organized. If ADHD sufferers can adjust their thinking patterns to stay coolheaded in the face of difficulty or dilemma, solutions will come to them as easily as they come to anyone else.

Coaching

Despite the fact that most health care professionals are only modestly familiar with coaching in relation to ADHD, coaching is a growing profession that is gaining in popularity due to its apparent effectiveness. The increased demand for ADHD coaching stems in large part from the fact that most adults who struggle with ADHD would like nothing more than to make adjustments that will alter their lives for the better; the problem often lies in follow-through, which is where coaches can help.

The coach-patient relationship is structured and goal-driven. The coach actively works with the ADHD sufferer to come up with practical strategies to maximize planning, organization, and pragmatism. Coaches begin by helping clients identify their goals, and then, like devising a game plan for a sport, helping them develop individualized strategies for achieving those goals. Coaching is highly individualized; for this reason, there is no standardized method used by all coaches. Coaches must be able to tailor strategies to the abilities and challenges of each client to effect positive changes.

Coaching differs from traditional therapy in that it emphasizes action rather than thinking strategies. It is goal-oriented, not philosophy-oriented. Coaching is about solving specific problems, together. In addition to giving their clients the first push toward identifying their goals in all areas of life—from daily tasks to work, love, and health—coaches typically take a more hands-on approach, giving their clients reminders, motivation, honest assessments of their progress, and, when necessary, "tough love" to keep them on track. Following in this model, coaches may ask clients questions that typically they wouldn't expect clinicians or therapists to ask. For example, coaches may call to ask their clients if they remembered to pay their bills, if they ate breakfast, or if they set up appointments for the coming week.

Clients are usually in regular contact with their coaches outside scheduled sessions. ADHD sufferers may be asked to report their progress to their coaches by phone or e-mail several times a week. The need to have something positive to report is often a very strong motivator.

Whereas therapy is regarded as a mode of treatment for ADHD, coaching focuses on improving well-being and quality of life. However, they're *not* mutually exclusive. Coaching can have limited benefits. Coaching can help clients learn basic skills such as creating time lines or daily schedules, but it is not as effective with people suffering from severe emotional or psychological problems. Clients who are not emotionally grounded or are still distracted by psychological turmoil may not be in a place in their lives to achieve the discipline needed to work with a coach. In these cases, patients can either seek traditional therapy before hiring a coach, or they can seek traditional therapy and coaching simultaneously to achieve combined benefits.

In any case, the effectiveness of coaching can ultimately be boiled down to the sheer number of achievements (no matter how small) a sufferer of ADHD can amass in a short period of time. Oftentimes, being able to identify and boast of goals that have been successfully met can speed a patient down the road to more, and even greater, successes.

Marriage and Family Therapy

ADHD exacerbates the everyday stress of modern life, and inevitably takes a toll on personal relationships. Furthermore, adults who have suffered with ADHD since childhood have a great deal of emotional baggage that is the unfortunate result of being fed negative messages over the course of a lifetime. Many of them have low self-esteem, issues with trust, and persistent fears associated with how their disorder may cause them to make mistakes throughout the day. It should come as no surprise, then, that people suffering from this disorder tend to have difficulty in their marriages, family, and careers.

When people are in constant contact or close proximity with one another, as family members or spouses tend to be, there is plenty of room for miscommunication and plenty of opportunities for feelings to get hurt. Someone who marries a sufferer of ADHD may initially take comfort in the idea that they can help their spouse. When this doesn't prove to be true after a prolonged period of time, disappointment and resentment can settle in. Members of an ADHD sufferer's family may tire of feeling responsible for "cleaning up" after the individual's mistakes and their attitude may begin to shift toward blame. Meanwhile, the ADHD sufferer feels as if she is a burden to others, or may begin to feel abandoned by the very people she believed would never give up on her. ADHD sufferers are often unaware of their symptoms and the resulting impact of their behaviors, which is why their relationships are often strained and why adults with ADHD are twice as likely to have been divorced (28 percent versus 15 percent) and/or separated (10 percent versus 5 percent).[1]

Marriage and family therapy can help by bringing these unspoken emotions to the surface. By engaging spouses and/or other family members, this type of therapy offers everyone involved the chance to better understand the disorder, to vent their frustrations, to alleviate blame, and to see the problem in a different light. Through mediating discussions and providing expertise, counselors can help spouses and family members realize that blame is not constructive. Typically, the counselor's goal is to shift the spotlight from the person with the disorder onto others. It becomes clear that relationship problems do not arise solely from the faults of the person with ADHD, but also from the spouse's or family members' inability to understand or exercise tolerance. When the responsibility for problems is shared, the process of collective healing can begin.

Group Therapy

Individuals who suffer from ADHD have usually spent much of their lives feeling different and inadequate compared to friends and coworkers. Feelings of alienation and social awkwardness may drive sufferers to avoid talking to people for fear that their "inadequacies" will be discovered. In fact, social impairment is a symptom criteria for ADHD. In a group therapy setting, where all participants suffer from the disorder, a person with ADHD can find the freedom to express him- or herself without fear of being judged. Simultaneously, they can find a pool of people from which they can select and make friends—something that a sufferer may find more emotionally difficult and riskier in the general population.

Group therapy can be a source of education, support, and acceptance for people whose ADHD has always made them feel misunderstood. By listening to the stories and frustrations of others who are dealing with the same difficulties, ADHD patients can come to see that they are not alone. They can also take great comfort in not only receiving support for their problems, but giving support to others as well. Discussions that occur during group therapy can also provide ADHD suffers with a forum from which they can gather and collectively develop coping strategies and symptom management skills. After employing these skills, they can share their successes with the group.

Perhaps one of the greatest revelations that group therapy can bring is that people with this disorder are just as intelligent, engaging, funny, attractive, and creative as anyone else. Knowing people to whom negative stereotypes associated with ADHD do not apply can help participants consider the ways in which they themselves excel as individuals.

EEG and Neurofeedback

Electroencephalography (EEG) is a controversial treatment used in recent decades as a treatment for ADHD, with varying results. Though the science of this method is rather complicated, EEG can be summarized as a way of measuring how certain brain waves react when different parts of the brain are charged with electrical currents, meant to simulate specific functions and activities. "Biofeedback" is the attempt to train individuals to modify their brain waves in certain situations, and "neurofeedback" is modification guided by the manipulation of electric currents.

Though initially EEG was used primarily to study the brain processes of people with ADHD, as noted above, attempts have been made recently to use it to *modify* brain processes and thus treat ADHD. This treatment is controversial and has generated much debate in the scientific community.

The basic goal of EEG biofeedback, neurofeedback, and neurotherapy is to train the ADHD patient to unconsciously decrease slow wave activity or increase fast wave activity in their brains. This is achieved through positive reinforcement. Patients undergoing treatment with EEG typically have one to three electrodes placed on their heads and connected to a computer. The electrodes read the patient's brain wave activity, and whenever a desired "normal" EEG pattern is detected by the computer, a monitor that the patient is watching gives a positive reward (usually points, like a video game). In theory, after many sessions of this type of training (usually twenty to sixty), the brain will learn to produce the desired EEG patterns on its own, thereby correcting the abnormalities causing the ADHD symptoms. This, of course, relies on the hypothesis that the patient will retain the ability to reproduce these brain waves readily outside the clinical setting after treatment stops.

Sufferers of ADHD who would like to consider EEG biofeedback as a treatment option should be warned that it tends to be expensive. Although it has shown promise in correcting ADHD in some patients (some studies showed improvements in academic achievement in children treated in this way), it is not fully clear that the improvements experienced were due to the neurofeedback and not to other factors (e.g., the increased time patients spent with therapists while undergoing EEG biofeedback treatment).[2]

Neurofeedback could be considered a treatment option for re-fractory patients who have experienced little success with stan-dard treatments.

You Make Your Miracle

In experimenting with complementary therapies, it is important to remember that, like pharmaceutical medications, they are not mir-acle workers. You may experience immediate positive changes, but more than likely progress will be slow. It's imperative that you don't give in to frustration and give up. Patience and persistence are key. There are many excellent treatments out there already, and new ones being discovered all the time; the right combination exists for you if you're willing to seek it out.

CHAPTER EIGHT

Alternative and Mind/Body Treatments

O f all the medications available by prescription, those meant to treat ADHD are among the best researched and understood. Their efficacies, as well as shortcomings, are well documented, and their side effects—when they occur—are usually manageable.

Even though the medications used to treat ADHD have been reviewed and studied extensively, some individuals would prefer to seek alternatives to prescribed medications.

What Are Alternative Treatments, Really?

Alternative treatments are so called because they represent "alternatives" to standard medical therapy. Physicians who believe in alternative treatments believe that ADHD is caused by chemical imbalances in the body and the brain, and that these imbalances can be corrected by ingesting the proper foods, providing the body with the proper balance of nutrients, and learning to control the imbalances using the power of the body and mind.

To date, there has been too little scientific research done to substantiate this theory or to measure the effectiveness of any of these treatments as true "alternatives" to traditional treatments for ADHD. Most in the medical field believe these treatments have little efficacy, but I believe consumers should be aware of them, so they can make up their own minds. Where there is research, I have provided citations for you to explore further. It is hard to argue against the substantial and life-changing effects of the standard pharmacologic treatments, which have withstood the rigors of scientific investigation for several decades. However, for those who would prefer to try a road less traveled, alternative treatments remain an option. The treatments described below are the most popular and most widely used alternative treatments for ADHD. Most have not been scientifically shown to improve ADHD symptoms and there have not been long-term studies. My general take on alternative therapies falls under the "Do no harm" dictum. Consider trying them if they "do no harm" and only in conjunction with your doctor's advice and counsel.

Diet and Nutritional Adjustments

DIET

Some individuals argue that eliminating certain additives or sugars in the diet helps ameliorate symptoms of ADHD. Unfortunately, there is little data to support this. Furthermore, although many people talk about having a "sugar high," scientific studies have not supported a link between increased simple sugar intake and ADHD symptoms. You should consult your physician prior to making any significant dietary changes. Again, if done under medical supervision, these dietary manipulations are not likely to cause significant harm and might help reduce ADHD symptoms, but again, there is not a substantial body of scientific evidence to support this. I recommend that patients eat a well-balanced, healthy diet that follows the FDA nutritional guidelines. Nothing can replace good nutrition, but this is a general prescription for all individuals and not specific to those with ADHD.

NUTRITIONAL SUPPLEMENTS

The use of nutritional supplements as an alternative treatment for ADHD is based on the idea that something is lacking in the diet of an ADHD sufferer, with the result being a chemical imbalance that causes symptoms to appear. Below is a partial list of a number of nutrients with some reported efficacy.

Essential fatty acids: Neuronal membranes in the brain are composed of phospholipids, which contain large amounts of polyunsaturated fatty acid. All complex biology and terminology aside, what is important to understand is that these fatty acids (mainly omega-3's and omega-6's) cannot be manufactured by the human body; it is, therefore, "essential" that we consume them. Preliminary evidence indicates that ADHD patients might have some imbalances of these particular fatty acids in their membranes, so in concept, consumption of these fatty acids (found in certain types of oily fish, such as salmon, and in flaxseed oil) can tip the imbalance in the right direction. It should be noted that some studies have shown that omega-3 and omega-6 fatty acids protect against bipolar disorder—a condition that can accompany ADHD.

Vitamins: Though various types of vitamin supplements have been recommended by health care professionals, the combina-

tion that has had the greatest verifiable success in mitigating
ADHD symptoms are multivitamin preparations based on the
"Recommended Dietary Allowances" (RDA) put out by the
National Research Council of the National Academy of Sciences.
Some studies have shown that taking these vitamin preparations
daily can result in higher concentration levels, faster reaction times,
and overall better performance in school and in work.

Minerals: The main candidates for mineral supplementation are
iron, zinc, magnesium, and calcium. Several small studies have
found levels of these minerals to be low in people with ADHD.
However, studies have not shown substantive scientific improvement with supplementation of these minerals. Consult your physician if you are considering taking these supplements in doses above
the recommended daily allowance.

Herbal Remedies

A variety of herbal remedies, including ginkgo biloba, hawthorn,
gotu kola, and rosemary, have been reported to yield cognitive
benefits to certain individuals. However, there is no scientific evidence that they have primary effects in ADHD, and side effects
when combined with standard ADHD medications are unknown.
Again, effects in the individual are possible, but it is "buyer be-
ware," as the long-term effects and benefits of herbal preparations
are unknown.

Traditional Chinese Medicine

Traditional Chinese medicine has been developed and practiced
for more than two thousand years. Prior to the introduction of

modern Western medicinal practices, Chinese medicine was the primary form of treatment throughout East Asia for illnesses. The dissemination of modern Western practices, however, has not replaced traditional Chinese medicine in China, Japan, or Korea. In recognizing the benefits of each school of medicine, Western and Chinese medicine are often used in conjunction to produce the greatest therapeutic effects for patients. There is evidence that the combined use of Eastern and Western medical practices is beginning to catch on in the United States. Some health insurance providers have started covering treatments such as acupuncture under their plans for the first time. However, as with other alternative treatments, their efficacy in alleviating the symptoms of ADHD has not been fully established.

Acupuncture

Acupuncture is one of the fastest growing forms of alternative treatment in the United States today. Its legitimacy continues to grow as modern scientific studies, in both the East and the West, have substantiated its effectiveness in treating a wide range of ailments. The practice involves strategically inserting thin needles (which is actually quite painless) into specific points on the body to balance *qi*, or energy flow, so that the body's ability to heal itself in specific ways is maximized.

Acupuncture has been used as a treatment for anxiety, depression, and stress disorders—all of which tend to co-occur with ADHD. In recent years, however, acupuncturists have developed treatments specifically to alleviate the symptoms of ADHD; I am not aware of long-term systematic studies examining the effectiveness of acupuncture in adult ADHD.

Mind/Body Treatments

In recent years, therapies in this category have grown steadily in popularity alongside alternative treatments as a whole. Mind/body treatments seek to create a stronger connection between the mind and the body, thus enhancing a person's ability to self-heal and control mood. Mind/body treatments are holistic approaches that are attractive for their complete lack of side effects, their overall health benefits, and, for many, the added bonus of their being fun to practice. In the case of ADHD, they are especially relevant because many have a natural focus on relaxation (which counters hyperactivity, anxiety, and depression) and concentration (which counters inattentiveness and mood swings). Though the fewest number of studies have been done on this category of treatments, mind/body therapies continue to grow in popularity, not just among sufferers of ADHD, but also among sufferers of other ailments for which traditional medicines have had disappointing effects. In the following list, the various mind/body treatments are divided into "bodywork" and "movement therapies."

Bodywork

EXERCISE

Though the general health benefits of leading an active lifestyle are undeniable, exercise may prove especially useful in managing the symptoms of adult ADHD. Though the debate continues over whether or not prolonged physical activity lessens the severity of psychological disorders over time, there is substantial evidence to show that at least in the short term, physical activity decreases hyperactive behavior and aggression, and significantly reduces stress.[1]

The effect of endorphins (which have been described as the "messengers" for our emotions) on the body has been well studied, and it is commonly known that the release of endorphins reduces pain and simulates feelings of happiness. Exercise, when done at the proper intensity, prompts the body to release endorphins in inordinate quantities. For patients who suffer from depression in addition to ADHD, engaging in a regular exercise routine can prove an effective way to manage negative feelings.

MASSAGE

Massage is deep-pressure stimulation of muscle tissue, typically used for its proven calming effects. One study showed regular massage improved short-term mood and longer-term behavior in a classroom setting.[2] Some people have reported reduced anxiety and activity levels immediately following massage therapy, as well as increased responsiveness.

MEDITATION

Meditation involves relaxing the body and allowing the mind to fall into a state of deep calm and focus through quiet and controlled breathing. Meditative practices are usually designed to cease wandering thoughts, and this can be achieved through postures (sitting with the legs and arms folded in certain ways) and focused visualization on a single image behind closed eyes. For ADHD sufferers who can achieve this state of calm, meditation can be rewarding.

The practice of prolonged and focused visualization during meditation can train the mind to maintain concentration—something patients with ADHD usually struggle with. Though meditation is inherently difficult for people who are prone to inattentiveness, testimonials from ADHD sufferers who have persisted in practicing meditation report that obtaining calm focus becomes easier.

Movement Therapies

Movement therapies are typically ancient mind/body therapies that originated in the East. Though their origins date back centuries or even millennia, and though they have been practiced in East Asia for ages, these practices have only recently gained widespread attention in the West for their therapeutic and health benefits. The most popular ones with ADHD patients are yoga and tai chi.

YOGA

Yoga employs the use of breathing techniques, postures, and cognitive control (meditation and relaxation) to alter the practitioner's state of mind. Though there has been no evidence that yoga directly benefits ADHD, it has been found to improve emotional states and significantly reduce anxiety. One recent study reported that after practicing yoga, many adults experienced less anger, tension, and hyperactivity.[3] These results may be attributable to yoga's proven effectiveness in reducing heart rate and breathing rate. Furthermore, several studies have shown that those who participated in more intense yoga sessions and with greater frequency (practicing it on their own as well as in classes) experienced greater easing of troublesome symptoms. As with meditation, yoga may be difficult for ADHD individuals with inattention and impulsiveness, but for those willing to try it, the rewards can be great.

TAI CHI

Tai chi is a soft (no-contact), meditative martial art that involves slow, controlled movements and regulated breathing. The effectiveness of tai chi in reducing stress has long been known and accepted. It has not been extensively studied as a treatment for ADHD, but some patients report a decrease in symptoms after practicing tai chi.

An Unfolding Mystery

Just as the discovery and development of new medicines in the area of ADHD continues to unfold, so too does our understanding of alternative treatments. With a healthy dose of skepticism, and the advice of your doctor, you might find some of these alternative treatments worth a try.

Arnold, LE. "Alternative treatments for adults with attention-deficit hyperactivity disorder (ADHD)." *Ann NY Acad Sci.* 2001 Jun:931:310–41.

You *Can* Feel Better

I hope you now have a better understanding of what attention deficit hyperactivity disorder is and how it affects your life and the lives of those around you. You also have learned that there are co-conditions that may or may not be present and that there are a range of scales and other diagnostic tests to assist you in getting the most accurate diagnosis possible.

The two most important facts that I hope you picked up in these pages are:

1. You're not alone—there are many other people who suffer from this condition.
2. There are successful ways of treating ADHD and managing your symptoms.

As you already know, I've spent many years studying adult ADHD and treating individuals who have the disorder. We've come a long way, both in diagnosis and in treatment, and I'm pleased to report that today your condition can be effectively managed, freeing you up to pursue your life as you wish. Medication has done wonders for symptom management, and psychosocial ancillary treatments have given many individuals the essential skills to improve their lives. *The bottom line is that you* can *feel better.*

If you haven't taken the ASRS Screener, I urge you to do so now. If it indicates that you have ADHD, make an appointment with your primary care physician or someone he or she refers you to for proper diagnosis. Take this book with you. If you feel your condition is not being given the consideration it deserves, find another doctor. There are many practitioners across the country who are very familiar with ADHD and can assist you in treating and managing the disorder.

Do not become discouraged by the treatment. It is not a magic bullet and you won't see your life transform overnight. Have the patience to find the right medication and the right dose. Be honest with your doctor and/or practitioner and make sure to continue taking the medication—even when you feel better.

Lastly, if your condition has affected your personal and/or family life, it is essential that you address it head-on. It won't be easy, but there is help available. Support groups and other resources are listed in the appendix. Reaching out for help, including therapy, is not an indication of failure on your part in any way. Rather, it is an essential first step. Treatment is available, and it is a powerful tool that can help you move forward in your life with greater success, a sense of well-being, and happiness.

Appendix

Where to Find Further Information and Help

Helpful Organizations/Support Groups

A.D.D. WareHouse
300 NW 70th Ave., Suite 102
Plantation, FL 33317
954-792-8100
954-792-8545 (Fax)
www.ADDWareHouse.com

ADDult Information Exchange Network (ADDIEN)
P.O. Box 1701
Ann Arbor, MI 48106

ADDult Support Network (for ADD Adults)
Mary Jane Johnson
2620 Ivy Place
Toledo, OH 43613

Adult ADD Association
1225 East Sunset Drive, Suite 640
Bellingham, WA 98226-3529
206-647-6681

American Academy of Pediatrics
141 Northwest Point Blvd.
Elk Grove Village, IL 60007
847-434-4000
www.aap.org

American Psychiatric Association
1000 Wilson Blvd., Suite 1825
Arlington, VA 22209-3901
703-907-7300
www.psych.org

American Speech-Language-Hearing Association (ASHA)
10801 Rockville Pike
Rockville, MD 20849-1725
301-897-5700

Attention Deficit Disorder Advocacy Group (ADDAG)
8091 South Ireland Way
Aurora, CO 80016
303-690-7548

Attention Deficit Disorder Association
1788 Second St., Suite 200
Highland Park, IL 60035
847-432-ADDA
www.add.org

Attention Deficit Disorder Association SR (ADDA-SR)
12345 Jones Rd., Suite 287-7
Houston, TX 77070
www.ADDA-sr.org

Attention Deficit Information Network, Inc. (AD-IN)
475 Hillside Ave.
Needham, MA 02194
617-455-9895

Attention Deficit Resource Center
Lawrence L. McLear, Ph.D., Director
1344 Johnson Ferry Rd., Suite 14
Marietta, GA 30068
800-537-3784

Children and Adults with Attention
   Deficit Hyperactivity Disorder (CHADD)
8181 Professional Pl., Suite 201
Landover, MD 20785
800-233-4050
www.chadd.org

Closer Look
Parent's Campaign for Handicapped Children and Youth
P.O. Box 1492
Washington, DC 20013

The Council for Exceptional Children
1920 Association Drive
Reston, VA 20191
800-328-0272

ERIC Clearinghouse on Handicapped and Gifted Children
Council for Exceptional Children (CEC)
1920 Association Dr.
Reston, VA 22091-1589
800-438-8841

Information Center for Handicapped Children
605 G St. NW, 2nd Fl.
Washington, DC 20001

Learning Disabilities Association of America
4156 Library Rd.
Pittsburgh, PA 15234

412-341-1515
www.ldanatl.org

The Learning Disabilities Network
72 Sharp St., Suite A-2
Hingham, MA 02043
617-340-5605

National Association for Gifted Children
1155 15th St. NW, Suite 1002
Washington, DC 20005
202-785-4286

National Center for Learning Disabilities (NCLD)
99 Park Ave.
New York, NY 10016
212-687-7211

National Clearinghouse for Professionals in Special Education
1800 Diagonal Rd., Suite 320
Alexandria, VA 22314

National Information Center for Children and Youth with
   Disabilities (NICHY)
Box 1492
Washington, DC 20013
703-893-6061 (Local)
800-695-0285

National Institute for Learning Disabilities
107 Seejkel St.
Norfolk, VA 23505
805-423-8648

National Network of Learning Disabled Adults (NNLDA)
808 West 82nd St., F-2
Scottsdale, AZ 85257

National Parent Network on Disabilities
1600 Prince St., Rm. 115
Alexandria, VA 22314
703-684-6763

Parent Advocacy Coalition for Educational Rights (PACER)
4826 Chicago Ave., South
Minneapolis, MN 55417
612-827-2966

The Parent Educational Advocacy Training Center
228 South Pitt St., Suite 300
Alexandria, VA 22314
703-836-2953

Professional Group for ADD and Related
    Disorders (PGARD)
28 Fairview Road
Scarsdale, NY 10583
914-723-0118

Other ADHD Books

ADD-Friendly Ways to Organize Your Life, by Judith Kolberg, Kathleen Nadeau (2003, Brunner-Routledge)

ADHD: A Complete and Authoritative Guide, by Michael I. Reiff, Sherill Tippins, and Anthony Alex LeTourneau (2004, American Academy of Pediatrics)

ADHD in Adulthood: A Guide to Current Theory, Diagnosis, and Treatment, by Margaret Weiss, Lily Trokenberg Hechtman, and Gabriel Weiss (1999, Johns Hopkins University Press)

Answers to Distraction, by Edward M. Hallowell and John J. Ratey (1996, Bantam)

Attention Deficit Disdorder: The Unfocused Mind in Children and Adults, by Thomas E. Brown, Ph.D. (2005, Yale University Press)

Attention-Deficit Hyperactivity Disorder in Adults, by Paul H. Wender, M.D. (1998, Oxford University Press)

Delivered from Distraction: Getting the Most out of Life with Attention Deficit Disorder, by Edward M. Hallowell and John J. Ratey (2005, Ballantine)

Driven to Distraction: Recognizing and Coping with Attention Deficit Disorder from Childhood Through Adulthood, by Edward M. Hallowell and John J. Ratey (1995, Touchstone)

Mastering Your Adult ADHD: A Cognitive-Behavioral Treatment Program (Treatments That Work), by Steven A. Safren, Susan Sprich, Carol A. Perlman, and Michael W. Otto (2005, Oxford University Press)

Out of the Fog: Treatment Options and Coping Strategies for Adult Attention Deficit Disorders, by Kevin Murphy and Suzanne Levert (1995, Hyperion)

Survival Tips for Women with AD/HD: Beyond Piles, Palms, and Post-its, by Terry Matlen (2005, Specialty Press)

Taking Charge of ADHD: The Complete, Authoritative Guide for Parents (revised edition), by Russell A. Barkley, Ph.D. (2000, The Guilford Press)

Understanding Women with AD/HD, by Kathleen G. Nadeau (2002, Advantage Books)

Women with Attention Deficit Disorder: Embracing Disorganization at Home and in the Workplace, by Sari Solden (1995, Underwood Books)

ADHD Resources, Books, Tapes, and Videos

(request a free catalog from the following)

The ADD Resource Center
1344 Johnson Ferry Rd., Suite 14
Marietta, GA 30068

A.D.D. WareHouse
300 Northwest 70th Ave., Suite 102
Plantation, FL 33317
305-792-8944

American Guidance Services (AGS)
4201 Woodland Rd.
P.O. Box 90
Circle Pines, MN 55014-1796

Developmental Learning Materials (DLM)
One DLM Pk.
Allen, TX 75002-1302

Free Spirit Publishing, Inc.
400 First Ave., North, Suite 616
Minneapolis, MN 55401-1724

Newsletters and Magazines

ADD Forum (CompuServe)
800-524-3388 (Representative 464)

The ADDed Line
3320 Creek Hollow Drive
Marietta, GA 30062
800-982-4028

ADDitude Magazine (for people who have ADD)
www. Additudemag.com

ADD-ONS
P.O. Box 675
Frankfort, KY 60423

ADDult News
c/o Mary Jane Johnson
ADDult Support Network
2620 Ivy Pl.
Toledo, OH 43613

The ADHD Report
Russell Barkley, Editor
Guilford Publications
72 Spring St.
New York, NY 10012
800-365-7006

Advance (a publication of ADDAG)
8091 S. Ireland Way
Aurora, CO 80016
303-690-7548

ATTENTION (magazine)
CH.A.D.D. National Headquarters
499 Northwest 70th Ave., Suite 308
Plantation, FL 33317
305-587-3700
www.CHADD.org

Attention Please!, Newsletter for Children
   with Attention Deficit Disorder
2106 3rd Ave.
North Seattle, WA 98109

BRAKES: The Interactive Newsletter for Kids with ADHD
Magination Press
19 Union Square West
New York, NY 10003
800-825-3089

CHADD Newsletters (CHADDER/CHADDER BOX)
CH.A.D.D. National Headquarters
499 Northwest 70th Ave., Suite 308
Plantation, FL 33317

HAAD ENOUGH
HAAD Support Groups
P.O. Box 20563
Roanoke, VA 34018

Kids Getting You Down?
Learning Development Services
3754 Clairemont Dr.
San Diego, CA 92117

The Rebus Institute Report
1499 Bayshore Blvd., Suite 146
Burlingame, CA 94010

ADD Resource Catalogs

ADD Books
P.O. Box 157
Dexter, MI 48130
313-662-2778

ADD Clinic
Resources for Parents
983 Howard Ave.
Biloxi, MS 39531
800-962-2673

ADD Discount Books
312 Riley Circle
Gadsden, AL 35901
334-543-1170

National Professional Resources, Inc.
Dept. C95, 25 South Regent St.
Port Chester, NY 10573
914-937-8879

Web Resources

One ADD Place
http://www.greatconnect.com/oneaddplace
(A virtual neighborhood that consolidates information and re-
    sources)

ADD Webnet

http://members.aol.com/addwebnet/index.html

(A central directory of links that connects you to sites of individuals or groups that provide information, offer support, or share insights on ADD)

ADD and ADHD Infoline

http://www.alcasoft.com/add

(Information and resources put together by a family's personal experience with ADD)

The NYU School of Medicine Adult ADHD Newsletter (for professionals)

http://www.med.nyu.edu/psych/psychiatrist/adultadhdnews letter.html

Colleges and Universities That Offer Programs to Help Young Adults with ADHD

American International College (MA)

Barat College of DePaul University (IL)

Beacon College (FL)

Brenau College (GA)

Chicago State University (IL)

College of Mount St. Joseph (OH)

Curry College (MA)

DePaul University (IL)

East Tennessee State University (TN)

Fairleigh Dickinson University (NJ)

Finlandia University (MI)

Illinois State University (IL)

Limestone College (NC)

Lynn University (FL)

Marshall University (WV)

Southern Illinois University (IL)

Texas Tech University (TC)

University of Arizona (AZ)

University of Colorado at Boulder (CO)

University of Denver (CO)

University of Illinois (IL)

University of the Ozarks (AR)

University of Wisconsin at Whitewater (WI)

West Virginia Wesleyan College (WV)

Western Carolina University (NC)

Notes

Chapter 1. What Is Adult ADHD?

1. J. Biederman and S. V. Faraone. "Attention-deficit hyperactivity disorder," *Lancet,* 366 (July 16, 2005): 237–48.

2. R. J. Kessler. "Prevalence of Adult ADHD in the United States: Results from the National Comorbidity Survey Replication (NCS-R)." Presented at the Annual Meeting of the American Psychiatric Association. May 2004, New York, NY.

3. Survey results presented at the American Psychiatric Association by Joseph Biederman, M.D., professor of psychiatry, Harvard Medical School, and chief of pediatric psychopharmacology at Massachusetts General Hospital, 05/07/04.

4. J. Biederman, S. V. Faraone, E. Mick, et al. "High risk for attention deficit hyperactivity disorder among children of parents with childhood onset of the disorder; a pilot study," *American Journal of Psychiatry* 152 (1995): 431–35.

5. J. Biederman and S. V. Faraone (2005): "Economic Impact of

Adult ADHD." Presented at the 158th annual meeting of the American Psychiatric Association. Atlanta: APA.

6. American Psychiatric Association. *Diagnostic and Statistical Manual of Mental Disorders,* fourth edition, text revision (Washington, D.C.: American Psychiatric Association, 2000).

7. Biederman and Faraone, "Attention-deficit hyperactivity disorder" (see chap. 1, n. 1).

Chapter 2. Not Just a Kids' Disorder

1. *Diagnostic and Statistical Manual of Mental Disorders (DSM-IV)* (see chap. 1, n. 5).

Chapter 3. Red Herrings and Red Flags

1. "Stimulants and atomoxetine in the treatment of ADHD," *J. Clinical Psychiatry Monograph* 19(1) (2004):2–3.

2. R. C. Kessler, L. A. Adler, et al. "Patterns and predictors of attention-deficit/hyperactivity disorder persistence into adulthood: results from the national comorbidity survey replication," Department of Health Care Policy, Harvard Medical School. *Biol. Psychiatry* 57(11) (January 1, 2005): 1442–51.

3. Stephen Faraone, et al. "Attention-deficit/hyperactivity disorder in adults," *Arch Internal Medicine* 164 (June 14, 2004): 1226.

4. A. Lenard, A. Adler, et al. "Training Raters to Assess Adult ADHD: Reliability of Rating." *Journal of Attention Disorders* 8 (2005): 121–26.

5. Faraone, et al. "Attention-deficit/hyperactivity disorder in adults" (see chap. 3, n. 3).

6. J. Biederman, T. Wilens, E. Mick, et al. "Pharmacotherapy of attention-deficit/hyperactivity disorder reduces risk for substance abuse disorder," *Pediatrics* 104 (1999): e20.

7. Biederman and Faraone, "Attention-deficit hyperactivity disor-
    der" (see chap. 1, n. 1).
8. S. H. Kollins, J. M. McClernon, and B. F. Fuenneler. "Association
    between smoking and attention-deficit hyperactivity disorder
    symptoms in a population-based sample of young adults," *Arch
    Gen Psychiatry* 62 (2005): 1142–47.

Chapter 4. What Causes ADHD?

1. Biederman and Faraone, "Attention-deficit hyperactivity disor-
    der" (see chap. 1, n. 1).
2. Ibid.

Chapter 5. Getting an Accurate Diagnosis

1. R. B. Millstein, T. E. Wilens, et al. "Presenting ADHD symp-
    toms and subtypes in clinically referred adults with ADHD."
    Journal of Attention Disorders 2 (3) (1997): 159–66.
2. *Attention-Deficit Hyperactivity Disorder in Children and Adults,*
    by Paul H. Wender, M.D. (2001, Oxford University Press).
3. Len Adler, M.D., and Julie B. A. Cohen. "Diagnosis and evalua-
    tion of adults with attention-deficit/hyperactivity disorder,"
    Psychiatric Clinics of North America 27 (2004): 187–201.
4. R. C. Kessler L. Adler, et al. "The World Health Organization
    Adult ADHD Self-Report Scale (ASRS)." *Psychological Medicine*
    35 (2) (2005): 245–56.

Chapter 6. Medications That Can Help

1. Robert Epstein, M.D., M.S., chief medical officer, Medco Health
    Solutions, Inc. "New numbers on ADHD in U.S. kids," WebMD
    Medical News.

2. T. E. Wilens, and T. J. Spencer. "The stimulants revisited." *Child Adolesc Psychiatr Clin North Am* 9 (2000): 573–603.

Chapter 7. Complementary Treatments

1.   Biederman and Faraone (see chap. 1, n. 3).
2. R. Barkley. "Attention-deficit Hyperactivity Disorder." *Scientific American* (Sept. 1998): 47.

Chapter 8. Alternative and Mind/Body Treatments

1. J. F. McGimsey, and J. E. Flavell. "The effects of increased physical exercise on disruptive behavior in retarded persons." *J Autism Dev Disord* 18(2) (June 1988): 167–79.
2. S. Khilnani, T. Field, M. Hernandez-Reif, et al. "Massage therapy improves mood and behavior of students with attention-deficit/hyperactivity disorder." *Adolescence* 38(152) (Winter 2003): 623–38.
3. B. G. Berger, and D. R. Owen. "Mood alteration with yoga and swimming: aerobic exercise may not be necessary," *Percept Mot Skills* 75(3 pt 2) (Dec. 1992): 1331–43.

Index

Resources: ASRS v1.1 Screener, 28, 107–8; books about ADHD, 176–79; catalogs, 181–82; Internet, 182–83; newsletters, magazines, 179–82; organizations/support groups, 171–76; symptom assessment scales, 108–9; tapes, videos, 178–79
Response to treatment, 142
Retrospective accounts, 117
Ritalin (methylphenidate), 43, 117, 126–27, 129, 133

Screening test for ADHD, 28–29, 103–8
Self-diagnosis of ADHD, 24
Self-esteem, ADHD and, 18, 153; psychotherapy and, 147
Self-management, ADHD and, 56–57
Self-medication, for ADHD, 18, 21; substance abuse as, 71
Self-referred adults, with ADHD, 122
Serotonin, 137–38
Serotonin reuptake inhibitors (SSRIs), 65
Side effects of medications, 127; amphetamines, 132, 133; Bupropion, 137; Strattera, 134; stimulants, 128; trycyclic antidepressants, 137, 138
Smoking, 17–18, 20, 71, 136
Social phobias, 69
Society, modern, and Adult ADHD, 49–50
SSRIs (serotonin reuptake inhibitors), 65
Standardized rating scales, 102–12
Stimulant medications, 43, 117, 125, 126–27, 128–33; cholinergic agents, 136; combination therapy, 139–41; effectiveness of, 144; sustained-release, 118. See also Medications; Non-stimulant medications
Strattera (atomoxetine), 8, 43, 52, 117, 119, 125, 126–27, 133–36, 139; dosage, 141–42
Stressful situations, and ADHD, 14–15
Studies of ADHD, 98
Substance abuse, 71, 73, 99, 100; ADHD and, 17–18, 19–21, 50, 63, 64, 66, 67, 120–21; medications and, 125, 128; in pregnancy, and ADHD of child, 81
Success, professional, ADHD and, 3
Suicidal thinking, Strattera and, 134

Support groups, 171–76
Sustained-release medications, 118; methylphenidates, 51–52, 95, 129–30, 131, 133. See also Medications
Symptom assessment scales, 108–9
Symptoms of Adult ADHD, 62, 91, 92–100, 116; checklist, 103–7; DSM-IV criteria, 25–26; medications and, 3; patients, 13–15, 19, 51, 64–66, 94–95, 97, 119, 130–31, 135–36, 139–40; self-report scale, 4–7

Tai chi, 166–67
Therapies for adult ADHD, 56
Tic disorders, medications and, 125, 128, 133–34
Tobacco, ADHD and, 17–18, 20, 71
Tofranil (tricyclic antidepressant), 126–27, 137
Treatment of Adult ADHD, 3, 27, 30–31, 32–33, 56; and comorbidities, 72–73, 95; medications, 8, 115–42; non-medical, 13, 143–57, 159–67; response to, 142; strategies, 121–22. See also Medications
Tricyclic antidepressants, 124, 126–27, 137

Underperformance, ADHD and, 20, 46, 50
Undiagnosed ADHD, xii, 22–24, 100
Universities, helpful programs, 183–84
Untreated ADHD, 17, 37, 48, 116; and substance abuse, 121

Venlafaxine (Effexor), 126–27
Videos, helpful, 178–79
Vitamin supplements, 161–62

Wellbutrin (bupropion), 65–66, 126–27, 137
Wender-Reimherr Adult ADD Scale, 108, 109
WHO. See World Health Organization
Women, and ADHD, 55, 116
Workplace, ADHD in, 51, 52–55. See also Employment
World Health Organization (WHO), 28; and ASRS v1.1, 4, 103

Yoga, 166